# LIBERATION THEOLOGY

Dec 1997

# Liberation Theology

AN IRISH DIALOGUE

Edited by Dermot Lane

GILL AND MACMILLAN

First published 1977 by
Gill and Macmillan Ltd
15/17 Eden Quay
Dublin 1
with associated companies in
London and Basingstoke
New York, Melbourne, Delhi, Johannesburg

7171 0862 7

Printed in Great Britain by Bristol Typesetting Co Ltd,
Barton Manor, St Philips, Bristol

# Contents

# Contributors

*Francisco F. Claver,* Bishop of Malaybalay in the Philippines. Qualified Anthropologist. Author of several articles on human rights and social justice. Member of the Papal Commission for Non-Believers.

*Garret FitzGerald,* Irish Minister for Foreign Affairs 1973-1977. Member of the Senate from 1965-1969 and Dáil Eireann (the Irish Parliament) since 1969. He is also a staff member of the Political Economy Department in University College, Dublin, currently on secondment. Publications include *Towards a New Ireland.*

*Dermot A. Lane,* Chairman of the Irish Theological Association. Prefect of Studies in Holy Cross College, Clonliffe, and lecturer in Theology in Mater Dei Institute of Education. Author of *The Reality of Jesus.*

*Enda McDonagh,* Professor of Moral Theology and Dean of the Faculty of Theology, Pontifical University of Maynooth. Published works include *Invitation and Response* and *Gift and Call.*

# Introduction

'Liberation Theology' is a label covering an important movement in theology which has come out of Latin America. Like most labels in life it has come to mean many things to different people. One of the reasons for this is that liberation theology has grown to maturity rather quickly. For some this is a reason for regarding it with reserve whereas for others it is an encouraging sign of the Church's ability to address itself to contemporary questions. The fact that liberation theology has grown up quickly does not imply that it did not experience the confusion which we normally associate with adolescence in the home. However, that adolescence is a thing of the past and liberation theology has become a vital issue in the life of the universal Church.

## What is Liberation Theology?

Liberation theology is the outcome of Latin America's response to the call by the Second Vatican Council to scrutinise the signs of the times and to interpret them in the light of the gospel. An examination of the historical situation in Latin America disclosed a situation of political domination and economic dependency. These realities were interpreted by faith as unjust and sinful. The struggle by Latin American Christians to free themselves from this oppressive situation gave rise to what is now known as 'Liberation Theology'.

The theology of liberation therefore is that which results from a critical reflection on Christian practice as inspired by the gospel. There is a sense in which this theology has grown out of a pre-theological commitment to social justice. Liberation theology does not start with God but with human beings in their concrete historical situations under the judgement of the gospel. It is within this perspective of practical experience and its relation to the gospel that liberation theology has come to see itself not only as a new way of *doing* theology but also as a way of liberating traditional theology from its apparent confinement to theory.

The goal of liberation theology is not simply to interpret the world but rather to change the world. It is not enough to know the truth; we must *do* the truth. The primary emphasis in liberation theology therefore is on *praxis* as distinct from pure theory. *Praxis* here should not be identified simply with blind practice. Rather *praxis*, properly understood, is the critical relationship that exists between theory and practice which influence and transform each other in faith. Indeed the measure of right theory (orthodoxy) is the extent to which it issues in right practice (orthopraxis).

The notion of truth with which the theology of liberation works is not that of the conformity of the mind to a given object. The world for liberation theology is not a static object which the human mind confronts and understands. Instead, the world is an unfinished project which is in the process of being built up by people. Theological truth is to be found in that liberating *praxis* of love in action which transforms the world into a more just and humane place in accordance with the divine promises enshrined in the Kingdom of God announced by Jesus Christ.

The purpose of theological doctrine according to liberation theology is to bring about a historical *praxis* that will promote justice and freedom. Most of all, liberation theology tries to incarnate through concrete action Christian faith, and hope, and love in history.

## Underlying Principles

This self-understanding of Latin American theology is based on fundamental underlying principles. These principles, at the risk of over-simplification, may be summarised as follows:

(a) *The World*: The basic faith uniting all theologians of liberation is that the world we live in is meant to be different. The world today does not exist in harmony with the divine plan of creation and salvation. The world however is capable of radical change. The Christian must play a vital part in bringing about this change in the world.

(b) *Sin*: The existence of so much deprivation and domination and dependency in the world today is the by-product of human selfishness and sinfulness. The effects of individual sin have become incorporated into structures of political and economic oppression. These sinful social structures must be changed through the establishment of a new economic and ethical order based on justice.

(c) *God*: The God of liberation theology is a God of the biblical tradition who is active with his people in their struggle for social justice. This same God continues to reveal himself today to people through the processes of Christian liberation.

(d) *Jesus Christ* :   Liberation is always a movement *from* the slavery of sin and oppression *towards* the freedom of human being before God. This process of liberation is bound up with the grace of salvation in Jesus Christ. Liberation is not an end in itself; it is a means, an essential means, towards the initiation of salvation in Jesus Christ.

(e) *The Church* :   For liberation theology the mission of the Church is to be an active sign/sacrament and credible witness of the salvation the Church proclaims. The Church does this not only by announcing the Good News in Word and Sacrament but also by engaging in a liberating *praxis* which will create a better world here and now. To this extent the Church must be prophetic. This implies speaking out against institutional injustice and spearheading action movements that will lead to social and economic change at the local, national and international level.

(f) *Consummation* : The theology of liberation realises that there will always be a necessary tension between that which has already been achieved historically and that which is yet to be realised as promised in the Second Coming of Christ. This tension between 'the already' and 'the not yet' is the creative source of imaginative Christian action for justice. Human efforts to create a better world through the process of liberation are understood as a 'foreshadowing of the new age' (*Gaudium et Spes* a.39) which is promised as absolute gift.

These developments in Latin American liberation

theology have been paralleled by equally significant statements which have been issued by the official teaching Church. It is not always easy to decide whether it was liberation theology that was influencing the teaching Church or vice versa. Perhaps it is nearer the truth to say that there was a mutual influencing taking place.

## Official Church Statements

While it is clear that liberation theology has grown out of a return to the Judaeo Christian prophetic tradition of the Bible, it must also be pointed out that the Church in recent times has become explicitly concerned about the same issues. Some would argue that this concern of the Church goes back to the social teaching of Pope Leo XIII. It is easier however to trace the development of liberation theology from the harvest of ideas that were reaped at the Second Vatican Council.

Among these ideas was the acceptance of the autonomy of the secular order (*G.S.* a.36), the recognition of human responsibility for the creation of a better world (*G.S.* a.34, *Apostolicam Actuositatem*, a.5, 7), and the emergence of a theology of earthly values (*G.S.* a.34, 38, 39, 43).

The implications of these ideas were spelt out by Pope Paul VI in *Populorum Progressio* in 1967. In that outstanding encyclical the world was reminded of the need to promote the integral human development of every person and of the whole person at the same time.

A year later saw the coming together of the Latin American Bishops in conference at Medellin, Columbia, 1968. This important meeting provided the *Magna Carta* for liberation theology. A new Christian confid-

ence, consciousness and courage was created in the
Latin American Church by this Conference. The Medellin *Conclusions* noted 'that the present historical moment
. . . is characterised by underdevelopment . . . alienation
and poverty . . .' which 'awakens attitudes of protest and
desire for liberation, development and social justice'
(10, 2).

This new awareness in the life of the Latin American
Church became felt throughout the universal Church.
In early 1971 Pope Paul in an Apostolic letter, *Octo-
gesima Adveniens*, to Cardinal M. Roy, marking the
eightieth anniversary of the encyclical *Rerum Novarum*,
issued a call 'to collective action . . . for a just and necessary transformation of society' (a.51).

This call was followed up by the 1971 International
Synod of Bishops which declared in its document *Justice
in the World* : 'Action on behalf of justice and participation in the transformation of the world fully appears to
us as a constitutive dimension of preaching the gospel,
or, in other words, of the Church's mission for the
redemption of the human race and its liberation from
every oppressive situation' (Introduction). The same
Synod went on to say that 'unless the Christian message
of love and justice shows its effectiveness through action
in the cause of justice in the world it will only with difficulty gain credibility with men of our times' (ch.2). This
discussion of justice in action, which in reality is what
liberation theology is all about, was continued during
the 1974 International Synod of Bishops. This Synod
drew together different ideas including those of development and liberation under the umbrella of evangelisation.
While there may have been words of caution expressed

at this Synod about certain imbalances in liberation theology, the overall thrust of the Synod strongly favoured the Church's explicit commitment to justice, liberation, development and peace as integral to evangelisation (*Evangelii Nuntiandi* a.30, 31). These doctrinal developments in the official teaching of the Church in turn gave rise to statements and pastorals by local hierarchies throughout the world. One thinks of the documents produced by the Bishops of the Antilles (1976), Brazil (1977), Canada (1977), Chile (1977), France (1974), Paraguay (1976), Rhodesia (1974) and the United States (1976), each of which take a strong stand in the name of justice as an essential element of the gospel.

These statements by the Church, universal and local, clearly endorse the spirit of liberation theology. They further indicate the fact that the language of liberation and its theology are part of the ordinary teaching of the universal Church. This is not to suggest that all is settled with liberation theology; there are still many questions to be solved.

## Urgent Issues in Liberation Theology

One such issue is how to work out more clearly the precise relationship that exists between human liberation and salvation in Jesus Christ. This particular question was discussed at the 1974 Synod in terms of the relationship that exists between development and evangelisation. In his address to the assembled Bishops of the Synod Pope Paul came as near as anyone to answering this question when he pointed out that 'there is no separation or opposition, therefore, but a complementary relationship between evangelisation and human progress.

While distinct and subordinate, one to the other, each
calls for the other by reason of their convergence towards
the same end : the salvation of man'. It could be argued
that this issue of the relationship that exists between
liberation and salvation mirrors a larger question, namely
that of the relationship that exists between the sacred
and the secular, the divine and the human. It was this
question that troubled the early Church in the first few
centuries of its existence. The terms of reference for
approaching this question were drawn up by the Council
of Chalcedon (451) in its treatment of the relationship
between the human nature and the divine nature in the
person of Jesus Christ. The horizon suggested by Chalcedon was one of 'unity within distinction'. The distinction in question was not one of separation but rather one
of involvement : 'without separation and without confusion'. Is it possible that this model might act as a norm
for working out the relation between liberation and
salvation, between human progress and evangelisation?

Another urgent issue arising out of liberation theology
is that of trying to work out the role of the Church in
social and political questions. If the Church remains
silent and inactive in the area of social and political
policy there is a danger that it will be promoting the
*status quo*. To do nothing is to appear to do something.
On the other hand, if it takes a particular socio-political
stance it will be charged with meddling in politics.

Again this issue was raised during the last Synod and
remains a question to be resolved in liberation theology.
Some suggested that a distinction be made between the
Church as Hierarchy and the Church as People of God.
Within this distinction it is argued that the Church as

People of God should become directly involved in political issues and that the role of the Church as Hierarchy is to stimulate such involvement.

Others, however, would argue that the Church as both Hierarchy and People should become involved in social and political issues as prophetic critic. This would necessitate the Church assuming a prophetic and critical stance in word and in deed towards all forms of injustice in society. Such a stance would not presume to provide concrete political solutions but it would demand a change from the inequalities that exist in the world. Over and above this second possibility there are those who recommend that the Church must go beyond protest and actually provide positive political solutions while realising at the same time that every particular solution is provisional and therefore merely constitutes a step on the way towards the realisation of God's Kingdom.

These then are some of the underlying principles, Church positions, and urgent issues within liberation theology today. They are intended as an introductory background to this collection of papers which were originally delivered at the Annual Conference of the Irish Theological Association in Clongowes Wood College, Co. Kildare, in January 1977. The purpose of this Conference was to examine liberation theology with a view to discovering what light it might throw on the possibility of developing an Irish theology of liberation. The Conference was addressed by a theologian—Dr Enda McDonagh, of Maynooth, a politician—Dr Garret Fitz-Gerald, Minister for External Affairs of Ireland, and a practitioner of liberation theology—Francisco F. Claver S.J., Bishop of Malaybalay, Philippines. At the last moment Bishop Claver was refused a visa by his government to leave the Philippines. This extraordinary fact in itself highlighted for the Conference the kind of oppressive situations that do exist in the world and which are desperately in need of liberation. Fortunately for the Conference however Bishop Claver managed to send the text of his lectures and they were ably presented by Fr Marcus Keyes, an Irish missionary from St Patrick's, Kiltegan, working in the Philippines. The Irish Theological Association, along with Trócaire, the Irish Catholic Agency for World Development, sent a telegram to the Philippine Embassy in London expressing 'its sense of outrage at the flagrant denial of the basic human right to freedom of movement enshrined in the U.N. Declaration of Human Rights'.

In his opening paper, Dr McDonagh outlines what he regarded as 'The Challenge of Liberation Theology'. He traces the emergence of the twin ideas of dependence and liberation within Latin America. Against this background he concentrates attention on the God of liberation theology. He suggests that the central challenge of liberation theology is the reconciliation of the God of the oppressed with the God of the oppressor. It is easy enough to see how the God of the Judaeo-Christian revelation is a God who was intimately involved and continues to be intimately involved with his people in their struggle for freedom. But where does that leave the God whom the oppressor worships, the God whom we in the first world worship, the God who is claimed by the dominant first world which is responsible for the dependent third world? This is a rather uncomfortable and disquieting question which suggests that we in the first world are just as much if not more in need of the liberator God of liberation theology to the extent that we have allowed ourselves to be complacent and unconcerned with the oppressor-oppressed state of affairs in the world today.

The next two papers by Bishop Claver are concerned with 'Proclaiming Liberty to the Captives'. In his first paper Dr Claver examines the concept of the global village as a way of analysing what is wrong and what is right about our world today. He then asks to what extent should the Church, and by the Church he means the Institutional Church, get involved in the political sphere. He answers that the Church cannot remain apolitical. He illustrates how the Church must become involved in politics by providing some concrete examples of what is being done in the Philippines at present. His first paper ends by outlining four interrelated functions that the Church must perform in creating a better world. These are : annunciation, denunciation, initiation, and support.

In his second paper Dr Claver spells out his understanding of the nature of the Church in its role of promoting development and liberation. He argues that the Church must begin to trust people more. To the extent that the Church does trust people it also begins to learn from people. He then focuses attention upon the need for greater participation, dialogue and co-responsibility within the Church today. The laity must be given a real share in decision-making : the more they share in decisions that lead to action the more committed they will be to working as a conscious people of God. He concludes his paper by proposing an attractive model of the Church as Communication.

Dr FitzGerald in his paper 'Political Structures and Personal Development' begins by noting that the passion for domination and acquisition is the root cause of much violence and inequality in the world today. This passion, however, is counterbalanced by an equally strong human instinct towards freedom and sharing. He examines the political options available for promoting personal development : liberalism, socialism, and pluralist democracy. He sees the pluralist democratic system as possessing the most merits though it falls short of the ideal. In spite of its drawbacks it provides the greatest possibility for personal development. To promote this personal development, democracy must encourage critical judgement and a constructive scepticism concerning conventional wisdom. This presupposes a highly educated democratic society. This in turn raises the important question whether the educational system in Ireland encourages a critical approach to life. In particular it poses questions for a system of denominational education which in the eyes of some sees itself simply in terms of transmitting a particular set of inherited Christian values. Our educational system ought to enable people to overcome the pressures of conformity and consumerism. This can only be done by promoting a spirit of healthy criticism and open enquiry. Dr FitzGerald concludes his paper by emphasising the importance of active participation by people in the political processes of the democratic system as a further element which is essential to personal development.

The final paper by Dr McDonagh raises the question of 'An Irish Theology of Liberation'. The primary requisite for such a theology is that it must grow out of

a critical faith reflection on the Irish historical experience, both past and present. This is the basic lesson that
Irish theologians can learn from the Latin American
liberation theology. History is the *locus* of God's self-
revelation. Dr McDonagh argues forcefully that it is only
when people become subjects, as distinct from objects, of
their own history and destiny that they will truly encounter the God of Israel and the God of Jesus Christ in
history. In making this proposal Dr McDonagh takes a
critical look at Irish history. He suggests that the present
historical divisions in terms of North and South as well
as Catholic and Protestant are due in no small measure
to the fact that these different communities in Ireland
have become objects rather than subjects of their history.
It is this regrettable fact that is even now perpetuating
the painful oppression of terrorism and violence in Ireland.

The real task, therefore, facing Irish theology is that
of enabling the Irish people to become subjects of their
own history so that they may begin to experience the true
Lord of history who both heals by liberating and liberates
by healing. It is hoped that the bringing together of these
papers will help towards that end in some small way.

In conclusion, as Chairman of the Irish Theological
Association I would like to thank the 1976 Executive
Committee who helped so much in the organisation of
this Conference. In particular a special word of gratitude
is due to the Secretary, Rev. William Cosgrave, of St
Peter's College, Wexford, and the Vice-Chairman, the
Rev. Raymond Moloney, S.J., of Milltown Park, Dublin,
both of whom were more than generous with their time
in making the Conference succeed.

Dermot A. Lane.

# I.

# The Challenge
# of 'Liberation Theology'

ENDA MCDONAGH

*Introduction*

The 'Liberation Theology' under discussion is that
which has emerged in Latin America during the past de-
cade. In treating it as a challenge I excuse myself from an
extended exposition of it, so readily available elsewhere,
and at the same time I lay aside an *exclusively* critical
approach to the theological methods and positions
adopted by such theologians as Gutierrez, Asmann,
Alves, Bonino, Ellacuria, Segundo, Dussel and others.
To discern and respond to the challenge may be more
useful, provided discernment and response are based on
a careful and critical study of the published work available. And the category of challenge transcends the
purely academic. Given its origins, methods and aims,
this theology issues a challenge to all Christians and
every Church in a way and to a degree not usually
associated with theological development.

The challenge can be identified only in part here.
And the European theologian or Christian can take
some comfort, in face of the difficulties posed for his
world, that Latin American theology of liberation, itself
an unfinished task, poses even more immediate and less

easily avoidable difficulties for the theologians and
Christians in that continent. Little comfort can be
derived from the superficial judgement that this is just
another of these fashions in theology, so many of which
have come and gone in the last century and indeed in
the last couple of decades. Even if it should not live up
to the radical and comprehensive claims made for it by
some proponents, the context in which it has emerged
will remain to challenge theologian and believer to provide a better theological analysis and a more Christian
response.

### The Particularity of 'Liberation Theology'

All real theology has its historical and cultural par-
ticularity which makes it relatively inaccessible to the
'outsider'. This merely underlines one of the permanent
tasks of theologians as they seek to penetrate the experience and reflection of Christian believers from first-
century Palestine to twentieth-century Latin America.
The task is made possible at all by certain discernible
continuities in historical and cultural context, in faith
experience and in methods and fruits of reflection between the 'outsider' who wishes to understand and the
'insider' who is to be understood. The 'outsider' student
of current Latin American theology can share a great
deal with the 'insider' in terms of language and of cultural, philosophical and theological traditions. The communications explosion has made possible the development
of a certain global culture and life-style, however limited
and shallow. Against this general background some
access to Latin American theologising is clearly possible
for the European theologian. And he is very quickly

aware of the more specific interaction at the level of biblical studies, for example, where the Latin Americans are clearly very dependent on the Von Rads of Europe, or at the level of systematic theology where the traditional European heritage is still valued and used and contemporary European theologians such as Rahner, Metz and Moltmann have had considerable influence. In the more distinctive Latin American theological entry into dialogue with economic, social and political analysis, the basis of that analysis and dialogue is frequently European and in particular Marxian.

All this provides some basis for understanding the theology of liberation, for discerning and responding to its challenge. Yet, it could also blind the European to the particular 'insider' quality of it as a critical reflection in faith on the enterprise of liberation of a dependent people, by a believer committed to and engaged in that enterprise. For all his good intentions, informed sympathy and common intellectual heritage, the European remains decisively 'outside' this enterprise of liberation and the critical reflection in faith which makes it possible and necessary. Perhaps the neglected faculty of Christian and theological imagination may come to his assistance. However, he will approach his task of discerning and responding to the challenge, humbly if critically, well aware of the obstacles to understanding which his own position in the affluent, dominant and 'oppressive' world creates.

## A Dependent People

A 'theology of liberation' presupposes a theology or at least a consciousness of 'dependence' from which liberation is necessary. This dependence is defined first of all in economic terms and in reaction to the development-underdevelopment model of the economic relationships, a model which prevailed in the 1950s and early sixties. The enthusiasm which the development model generated in its early days rapidly turned sour as it failed to close the gap between the impoverished peoples of Latin America and the affluent of North America, Europe and Japan. The disappointment in practice was reinforced at the analytic and theoretical level by the conclusion that the model was essentially defective because 'underdevelopment' was the shadow side of 'development'. Development, according to this analysis, had succeeded and would succeed so long as there were 'underdeveloped' peoples to exploit for raw materials, cheap labour and consumer markets. 'Dependent' therefore was a more apt description of the deprived masses of Latin America than 'underdeveloped' or 'developing' with their suggestion of eventual development after the manner and to the degree of the already developed. Liberation from this dependent condition and not development has become the economic, political, social, moral and Christian imperative for these people. And the 1968 Conference of Latin American Bishops at Medellin gave at least some official recognition to the term and concept of liberation.

This very crude summary of the emergence of the twin ideas of dependence and liberation does scant justice to the actual conditions of poverty and oppression under which the mass of the people live; to the complex history of political colonialism and subsequent economic neo-colonialism with all their social and cultural consequences, to which these people have been subjected over the centuries; to the political, social and economic analyses which provide the immediate intellectual justification for the use of the terms. However, the immediate Christian challenge, as the Medellin conference indicated, is to take the side of the impoverished and oppressed. Peruvian theologian, Gustavo Gutierrez, spells out this commitment in terms of solidarity and protest. And it is within the perspectives of this identification with the poor and engagement in their cause that liberation theologians undertake their reflections. Here they find their distinctive *locus theologicus.*

## The God of Liberation Theology

It may appear a fairly banal discovery that Christian concern and engagement must be with the deprived and oppressed. It is perhaps less banal to follow that through by attempting to theologise from within the perspectives of the deprived and oppressed; in other words to discern through critical faith-reflection the activity and hence the nature of the God of Jesus Christ. Although the contemporary stress, among liberation theologians also, is through anthropology to theology, through man to God (in accordance with the example and person of Jesus Christ), the ultimate and central concern of Christian theology remains *the God* of Jesus Christ. And diverse human situations (at the reflective level, anthropological stances) inevitably offer very diverse perspectives on God as he reveals himself, gives himself to mankind. This seems to me the basic challenge of liberation theology: how can we reconcile the God of the oppressed with the God of the oppressor? Particularly, if we Christians of

North America and Europe must be classified as oppressors all!

Without shirking that challenge, which may well be dissipated by elaboration, it is necessary, if difficult, to share more fully the perspectives of the oppressed and their view of a God concerned with man, with man in his historical misery and dependence, his actual condition as they experience it. Of course a God unconcerned with their actual condition, or only concerned that they suffer it through to some post-historical consolation, can hardly be expected in turn to be of concern to them as they seek to transform their dehumanised world. Marxists have learned and taught that lesson well. But such a God could hardly be the God of the Bible, the Creator-Covenant God continually concerned for man in his actual historical condition and at a point when a trans-historical fulfilment was beyond man's ken. And he could hardly be the God of Jesus Christ, God-made-man, who so loved man-in-his-world. The God of Christians is concerned with man in his historical, human conditions or he is not concerned with him at all. By becoming man God became fully historical in fulfilment of his historical activity with and promises to the people of Israel. He remains historical, concerned and able to relieve the historic enslavement of man. From the perspectives of the dependent people of Latin America as from the perspective of the enslaved Israelite people in Egypt, he offers himself as a liberator God. The theologians of Latin America frequently stress this parallel. For them and their people it is not only a parallel but a sign and interpretation of God's continuing liberating work. And faith in that God is by entry into his liberating work, by taking his side with the oppressed and enslaved.

It is difficult to resist the urgency and sweep of this vision, although many individual obscurities and difficulties remain. Some of these will be discussed later. Here it is important to return to the perspective of the 'oppressor' consciously or unconsciously so , freely or 'helplessly' so. Accepting for the moment the model dominant-dependent, even in its extreme (realistic, some would argue) expression of oppressor-oppressed, one faces the critical question of what kind of God the oppressor worships. Obviously one can oppress while crying 'Lord, Lord'. But is this recognition of the God of creation, covenant, salvation in Jesus Christ or the substitution of some ideological idol? It is hard if not impossible to reconcile acceptance of the God of Jesus Christ, Yahweh of the *anawim* of Israel, the liberator God of Exodus with oppression or exploitation of a conscious and free kind. It is what these men do, not what they say, which is decisive. *Orthopraxy* is a surer guide to the reality of one's God than *orthodoxy*!

Do such conscious, free oppressions and exploitations occur? Oppression and exploitation certainly do in obvious and directly personal and physical ways but more pervasively and subtly, according to this analysis, through the economic, social and political structures whereby two-thirds of the world's population (and perhaps a still higher percentage in Latin America) are deprived of basic needs of food, clothing, shelter, education, and of any control over their own destiny. To endorse these structures is to play the role of exploiter or oppressor. To accept them or even ignore them, to refuse or neglect to join the struggle to transform them are all ways of identifying with the exploiter against the exploited and so with the 'God' of the exploiter against the 'God' of the exploited. The challenge to theologians, Church leaders and Christians as a whole in the Latin American situation is crystal clear for these analysts. Their challenge to the same categories in our world would seem to be no less profound, although obscured by distance in perception of it and blunted by the structural complexity in response to it.

The 'dependent' people are to be found not only in the Third World. Within the affluent countries there exist groups, classes—even races—who are also deprived and exploited through structural dependence. The liberator God would be more readily accessible to the privileged by their identifying first of all with their own deprived. The crucial irony is uncovered by the realisation that ultimately the privileged are also the deprived, the apparent masters also enslaved. We the dominant ones may be more in need of the liberator God and liberation theology than the dependent people of its origins. More in need, because we have invested so much of ourselves in the exploiter 'God'. In our comfort, we have so little incentive to unmask him; in our blindness so little insight into his falsity.

## *The Methods of 'Liberation Theology'*

The radical character of the challenge of liberation theology, as I discern it, is only fully realised by raising the ultimate question of God, although as an 'outsider' I may well have misinterpreted the intentions of these theologians, who do not present the challenge in quite the same terms. A more obvious if less basic challenge to the professional theologian emerges from their manner of doing theology. With a programme of critical faith-reflection on action these theologians remain within the general tradition of Christian theology. Theology must always in its reflection follow faith-experience and faith-action. However, that experience and action have hitherto been largely, but not exclusively, defined in religious or sacral terms. At any rate they have not been considered in primarily political terms. The primacy of action, and of political action at that, provides a very distinctive characteristic of liberation theology. Action precedes knowledge or at any rate theological reflection. Praxis, usually translated in terms of commitment to and engagement in the liberation of the dependent and marginalised peoples, has the primacy over theory, although clearly interaction of a dialectical kind is recognised. Orthodoxy is not simply replaced by orthopraxy, but a clear shift has taken place.

How far the theologians we read are actually engaged in the liberation process or 'making the revolution' as it is sometimes called, one cannot assess at this distance. Yet their commitment is undoubted and the validity claimed for their reflection rests on some involvement. Their starting-point therefore sharpens in methodological terms for the Western theologian, the basic challenge about God. The methodological challenge to him is sharpened still more by their employment of economic, social and political analysis as the first stage in critical reflection. The role played by philosophy or psychology in Western theology is replaced by the study of economics, sociology and politics, mainly of a Marxian kind.

To many 'outsider' theologians this may appear as the most disputable and least convincing element in the work of the liberation theologians. Yet they pose two very crucial questions to the 'outsider' : Does not every theology embody, unconsciously, some social, economic and political stance which would be better made explicit? What better alternative to the Marxian analysis is there available to deal with their 'dependent' situation? While these are extraordinarily searching and difficult questions for the outsider to answer satisfactorily, he may in turn feel free to pose a couple of his own of an equally practical kind : Where in the world has the Marxian analysis and the political engagement it promoted actually led to the liberation of a dependent people and not to a new form of slavery? If orthopraxy is prior to orthodoxy as a test of truth, how far has it been applied to the Marxist countries we know? These are not just *ad homines* arguments and reflect the concern and not just the threat which the methods of liberation theology provoke. The Latin American theologians must be well aware of such questions and must feel continually challenged by their own theological search and its provisional conclusions.

*Liberation in History: Insights and Obscurities*

The liberation advocated in this programme operates at three interrelated levels : the immediate economic, social and political level, the level of mankind's maturity in history and the theological level of liberation from sin into full authentic love-relationships with God and the neighbour. The insight gained here into the social and historical character of sin, its objectification in historical structures and the liberating activity of God in history

whereby man is called and enabled to become more
fully himself as the subject of his own history and the
master of his own destiny, is more readily shared with
the European theologian who is struggling with many
of these ideas himself. The contrast posed between the
'History of Salvation' and the 'Salvation of History' or
the insistence on the unity of all history in its finality in
Christ, can find origins as well as echoes in Europe and
North America. And the difficulties about preserving
some 'duality' between God and man, eschatology and
history, theology and anthropology, 'transcendence' and
'immanence' without falling into dualism, are not finally
dissipated North or South. There are more clear-cut but
no less tricky challenges concerning the distinctive mission
of the Church : the relation between 'evangelisation' and
'liberation'; the identification of the Church and not just
Christians with a political programme and eventually a
political achievement; and finally the unity of the Church
if it is to include people of very disparate political allegiances. But these are challenges to which a theology in
such an early stage of development could not be expected
to offer a final response. It may however be worth record-
ing in a spirit of enquiry some nagging European fears,
however much like 'outsider' talk they appear. The
dangers of a new socialist Christendom, whereby the
Church would again be too closely allied with the govern-
ing elite, cannot be readily dismissed. (The need for a
strong central government at least in the early stages is
occasionally mentioned.) Perhaps more developed ideas of
the 'state' in its distinction from 'society' are needed here
with a corresponding rethink of the Church's mission in
society, sharply distinguished from and sometimes in

opposition to the work of the state. Along this line there may be need not only for the mediation of a utopian vision between theological insight and political achievement but also for a much more concretely based and developed social ethic.

It may seem even more presumptuous for somebody from the 'successful' Western world to ask how far theologians in the impoverished and oppressed world of Latin America have made allowance for ultimate failure of the enterprise of liberation. Of course there is no easy assumption that success is at hand or will be achieved in the near or even medium-term future or that it will be achieved without much pain, suffering, death and temporary failure. But could there be final historical failure? And what kind of God would that suggest? The God of Jesus Christ? Perhaps these questions are no less properly addressed to ourselves in the affluent world. They remain, I believe, part of the exhilarating challenge posed by the Latin American theologians who in their commitment and reflection provide inspiration as well as challenge.

B

## 2.

# Proclaiming Liberty
# to Captives
# I: The Proclaimer

FRANCISCO F. CLAVER S.J.

*The Global Village*

The gift of the gab, I understand, is an Irish grace.
And phrase-making is a national pastime. This may all
be blarney, but blarney with a purpose. That is very
Irish too, I think. So I will start with a phrase that an
Irishman must have coined: the *global village.*

It is a made-to-order phrase on which to conveniently
hang the subject of this paper—the Church's role in the
promotion of justice and peace, of development and
liberation in the world today; her specific contribution
to the creation of a better world. For before we can ask
what the Church is supposed to do, we have to first
consider what that world is that is to be made better.
The idea of the 'global village', I think, is as good a concept as any to start with.

It is a happy phrase, pregnant with promise and meaning, yet for that very reason elusive and frustrating. For
the reality it connotes *is* and *is not* at the same time. *It is*
—because in a very true sense the world we live in has
shrunk tremendously, and nations and peoples are neighbours to one another in a way that was not possible in
the past. All this, thanks to modern means of communi-

cation. But at the same time, *it is not*—because the implications of that very neighbourliness are still not understood, its potential unrealised. And it seems to me it is this very problem of our world being and not being a global village that the Church must confront. That very confronting will, I believe, help define for us the role of the Church that we are interested in here.

For the term *global village* describes in a shorthand way what is wrong and what is right about our world today. The developed nations seem to have too much of the 'global' in them—and this is their strength as well as their weakness. The underdeveloped nations, on the contrary, are too much 'village'—and this too is their strength *and* weakness. These are over-generalisations, I know, but there is a grain of truth in them somewhere which can bear an attempt at further explication.

The Western world, the developed nations, have too much of the 'global' : I am thinking not only of political and economic power—the overt political imperialism of the past, the economic stranglehold of the present—that they possess, world-embracing both, people-crushing; but I am thinking also, and more especially, of such problems as arise from what social scientists call mass-cultures, production-line societies, and their attendant problems : a general aimlessness about life, depersonalisation, *ennui*, a surfeit of wealth or a preoccupation with its increase, the big city, urbanisation gone wild, to name a few.

The underdeveloped nations, on their part, have too much of the village : they are bogged down by tradition, hampered by struggles for power among petty kings and chieftains, too engrossed in internal problems to be able to see, or get involved in, the wider problems around

them, economically and politically dependent, struggling
to get out of their colonial past yet forever falling into
the mistakes of that same past.

We could continue to catalogue the differences between these two worlds of development, drawing up their
contrasting features and setting them against each other
in an almost infinite series. But whatever the result of
such an undertaking might be, it remains clear to me
that both worlds suffer from the same problem : myopia
and selfishness. That is probably an extreme generalisa-
tion. Let it be that—for the moment. Here I would like
to go a little into the underpinnings of this judgement,
trite and simplistic as it may seem.

BISA *1974*

Back in February and March of 1974, the first Bishops'
Institute of Social Action (BISA)—a programme worked
out by the Office of Human Development under the
Federation of Asian Bishops (FABC)—was held at
Novaliches, a suburb of Manila in the Philippines. The
Institute was geared towards making bishops critically
aware of social realities, towards helping them to face
up to social problems later in their own respective
dioceses and countries. It was an international gathering
of bishops and a sprinkling of priests and religious, forty
in all, from Burma, Cambodia, Laos, Singapore, Thailand, Indonesia and the Philippines.

The Institute lasted for two weeks. I will not give here
a blow-by-blow account of the process and development
of thinking that went on among the bishops (some may
deny the presupposition that bishops are capable of
thinking at all), but early in the first week we did zero

in on modes of development. At one point the question was starkly posed this way : 'Would not the development that we are speaking of here be tantamount to making our people simply more selfish?' Nobody was more startled by the question as it evolved from their own searching than the bishops themselves. A good number of us were Southeast Asians. The diversity of cultures we represented was certainly great, but if there was one aspect of Southeast Asian cultures that we could say was common to all of them, it would be the high valuation of family and the consequent emphasis on interdependence. Development would, it seems, run counter to these values : for the model of development that is being followed willy-nilly in most countries of Southeast Asia is a Western one, strongly capitalistic, almost exclusively profit-oriented. Could we accept a model that, for all practical purposes, meant rampant selfishness, stemming from what was in effect a short-sighted economic vision that saw only as far as one's profits allowed one to see?

In further discussions we came to a consensus that some kind of socialism would have to figure prominently in whatever models we would ultimately decide on. At this point in the Institute, I must say the Chinese experience gripped us in a fascination that most of us had never felt before. Towards the end the question became : can we help bring about a better world for the masses of Southeast Asia following the Chinese model—but without the repression of basic human rights and the sacrifice of lives that we associate with Mao's reforming experiment? Was there an Indonesian or Cambodian or Burmese or Thai or Filipino way of development, respecting our diverse cultural identity—yet thoroughly

Christian (or Muslim or Buddhist)? And in this Christian and ethnic model, in consideration of Maoist China's example, was there a place for Marxism?

We asked that question in 1974. We are still asking it. Meanwhile events are passing us by. South Vietnam, Laos and Cambodia are now under Communist rule. Dire prognostications are being made about Burma, Thailand, Indonesia, even about the Philippines turning Communist in a matter of years. And we continue to speculate and argue among ourselves whether one can be Christian and Marxist at the same time. (Somehow no one talks about whether one can be Christian and Capitalist in the same manner.) It seems this is all we are allowed to do as Church. We can speculate as much as we like, but the premises of our speculation are already laid down by official Rome. We can speculate; but we cannot act on the fruits of our speculation (even within the narrow limits set for us by our 'official' theology). Acting would be politics, and the Church does not engage in politics.

## *The Philippine Situation*

Let me bring this whole discussion down to a more concrete level. I refer here to the Philippine situation, a very particular case, true, but in many ways representative of other Southeast Asian nations and the Church in those far-flung regions.

A hard issue at this very moment—to both the Church and the government, to the people at large too—is the role religious and bishops have been playing in the political sphere. For the past four years, the country has been under martial law (an unsubtle attempt at investing a dictatorship with the trappings of constitutionality). Practically every human and civil right has been thrown overboard—or at least has suffered in some way—in the name of the 'emergency' which, believe it or not, has been invoked to develop by intimidation a new society of Filipinos. The bishops as a whole have been relatively silent. They have issued statements, it is true, on the general political situation, but their statements have usually been nothing more than—statements. The religious Superiors, on the other hand, both men and women, have as an Association taken the bishops' statements seriously and over the years have tried to put them into programmed action. They have been quite effective. So there has been conflict since—with the bishops and with the government.

During 1975 the Association of Major Religious Superiors of the Philippines (AMRSP) received a strong reprimand from the Congregation of Religious in Rome castigating them for their 'exclusively socio-political orientation'. A year later they received another letter, even stronger than the last, this time from two Roman Congregations: that of Bishops and that of Religious. So far there has been no threat of excommunication.

The point at issue seems to be this: To what extent can religious and priests—the Institutional Church, that is—involve themselves in the political sphere? It is a difficult question. If we take traditional Church action as a guide, we have an answer of sorts: When government tampers with sexual morality, pushes, for instance, a population control programme that makes extensive use of artificial means of preventing conception or seeks to liberalise divorce laws, the Church speaks out as a matter of course, does everything in her power to safeguard the purity of her teachings on human sexuality. There is a second instance : When government tries to enact legislation prejudicial to Church institutions—schools, hospitals, seminaries, convents, etc.—she cries out in the name of religious freedom. Nobody brings in the objection then that we, the Church, are meddling in political affairs. If the AMRSP had made this their answer, I doubt if they would ever have been privileged to receive those letters from Rome.

But is this answer enough? Is it an answer at all? I do not think so. It would mean reducing the Gospel merely to sexual morality and the preservation of institutional relics—not that I would deny the value of these. What about justice, social and individual, and the protection of human rights? What about the humane exercise of government itself, the rightful use of political power? What about economic development and the equitable sharing in its fruits? And lastly, what about the integration of all these into what we all too glibly call total human development? I wonder—would you also get letters from Rome if you started to involve yourselves in these questions?

## The Bishops of the Philippines

There is a group of people in the Philippines who have been supportive of the AMRSP but who, at least until recently, had not received any letters of warning from Rome : bishops. Seventeen of them, out of a total of seventy-six or so active pastors of dioceses, recently brought out a document of their own in which they set forth what they had thought out together to be the rationale of their political involvement. Here is the full text of their statement on this subject. I think it does set forth, succinctly and in an orderly manner, what our current thinking in the Philippines is on the subject at hand :

*Our Political Involvement: Its Rationale.* From conversations and discussions among ourselves, but more importantly from our actual pastoral approach in our respective dioceses and prelatures, we believe we have arrived at a common way of looking at things, of thinking and acting, a common way of preaching Christ's Gospel in the Philippines of today. We are painfully aware that not all will see eye to eye with us on what we feel are Gospel imperatives, nor on how we interpret those imperatives. But we trust anyway that the honest discussion of the premises we operate from will at least lessen tensions, lead to greater mutual understanding, perhaps even tolerance, and lay the groundwork for the unity that we must all strive for in the Lord.

(a) *Our Notion of the Church.* We start with our notion of the Church. For in the final analysis the different approaches we take with regard to martial law and its dictatorial form of government comes down to how we understand the Church, even more crucially, how we operate pastorally from this basic understanding.

To us the Church is not only *Institution*, jealous of its authority, of its prerogatives and rights. It is also *People* —the People of God, the Community of Believers. It is easy enough to accept this definition—as it is easy to accept the documents of Vatican II from which the definition is drawn, in which it is enshrined. It is not too easy making it a living reality. For if we are serious about the people-part of our definition, we will have to pay more attention to their life situation, to their life problems, to events that help—or do not help—them to live a more human and

Christian life. We do not deny the supremacy that the
spiritual must have in the life of Christians. But accepting
that supremacy does not mean that we neglect the physical. The Church is people, not simply souls, disembodied,
incorporeal. The Church is living men and women, flesh
and blood, of the existential present. It is they who must
live—and give witness to—the Gospel in the concrete realities of the Philippines today. Our preaching must take in
those concrete realities.

(b) *Our Political Involvement.* Hence our concern with
martial law and what it is doing to our people. This concern, we are told, is none of our business. Martial law,
dictatorial regimes, the running of government—these are
political matters, alien to preachers of the Gospel, outside
of their competence as men of the cloth. We disagree.

It is a paradox, but it seems to us that the less involved
in politics the Church professes to be, the more it is actually
involved—but in a way that is most detrimental to its
primary task of preaching the Gospel. For silence can mean
condoning political oppression. We cannot conceive of a
Church that preaches a Gospel which has nothing whatso-
ever to tell people in the political aspects of their life.

Affirming this, we are not advocating the entry of ourselves as Churchmen into politics pure and simple, into the
wheeling and dealing of politicians, into the manoeuvrings
for power that characterise the political arena. But there
are moral dimensions to the art and practice of government and we as Church must at all times be ready to
preach the principles of those moral dimensions. It is a
fact that under the restrictive conditions of martial law,
we, as pastors of our flocks, have grown in our understanding of our pastoral role in regard to the political aspects
of the life of our people. And we see clearly it is not
Christian for us to remain a-political.

(c) *Human Rights and Working for Justice.* It is in the
area of human rights and justice especially that we see the

unchristian nature of non-involvement. For the sad fact is, under martial law in the Philippines our people have been deprived of rights that are theirs simply because they are human : rights to freedom of speech, of association; rights to due process, to meaningful participation in decision-making processes touching their common welfare; rights to truth and information; rights even to their dignity as thinking men and women. In the government's frenetic drive towards economic development, these rights are of secondary importance. This we believe is a massive in-justice, compounded by deceit and wholesale manipulation of people, by the dehumanising fear that comes with the power of the gun.

In this immoral tampering with the lives of millions, should we as pastors be silent? Should we not 'rock the boat' on the plea that we are not to engage in politics? Or, base thought, because in speaking out, we will be losing privileges accorded the Church by the State; we will be endangering the continuance of our traditional institu-tions—schools, hospitals, radio stations, other apostolic projects?

(*d*) *Church Pronouncements.* We believe the answer is a resounding NO. It cannot be otherwise. We have our very words as a Conference to go on. Our many statements over the years on social questions point clearly in a definite direc-tion of deep social concern and involvement. We have the FABC statement of Taipei in 1974 and its call for a 'dia-logue of life' with the people of Asia. We have the ringing declaration of the Asian Bishops' Meeting in Manila in 1970 and its brave stand of fighting injustice wherever, whenever, by whomsoever it is committed. We have the statement on human rights of the Synod of 1974 and the document on justice in the world of the Synod of 1971. We have Papal pronouncements galore from *Evangelii Nuntiandi* to *Populorum Progressio*, and even farther back to *Mater et Magistra.* And, finally, we have the documents of Vatican

II, *Gaudium et Spes* and *Lumen Gentium* especially, with
the full authority of the Council behind them.

We are not adducing these documents and statements
merely to support the stance we have taken. Rather it is
to ask : since they are *our* words—or at least we as Bishops
occasionally mouth and quote them—what do we mean by
them? What do they mean for our people?

(*e*) *Our Credibility.* From what we have said above
about our notion of Church, about political involvement,
about human rights and justice, we answer our own questions : we take seriously the social teachings of the Church.
We do mean the words we have spoken ourselves as a Conference of Bishops. And we try to translate them into pastoral programmes which speak to people directly where they
are. It is only thus, in our suiting of deeds to words, that
our message will have meaning for ourselves and our
people.

But precisely because we try to put beautiful words into
effective execution, we become 'destroyers of the peace',
'sowers of the seeds of discord'. We fear the greatest problem facing the Church today in its task of evangelisation
is its general lack of credibility as a witness to the Gospel.
And we, Bishops of the Philippines, are not helping towards the filling of that lack. We say one thing. We do
another. Or at least we are content to confine our preaching to the pulpit. We are afraid to descend to where our
people live their lives—the marketplace, the highways and
by-ways, the farms and barrios. We wonder if this is what
the Synod of 1974 and *Evangelii Nuntiandi* mean by 'integral evangelisation'.

## The Role of the Church

As the bishops themselves say, their thinking on the
question of the Church's involvement in political questions is the fruit not only of speculation but of actual

pastoral practice in their own dioceses. Their reasoning is cyclic. They start out with their notion of what the Church is. Accepting the Church as people of God as well as institution, they assert the need to be concerned with the life problems of people. In the Philippines, issues of justice and human rights and inequitable development loom large among those life problems. Hence their full involvement in them. They cite current Church pronouncements supporting such involvement and end with the notion of Church again, but this time with soul-searching questions about her credibility as a witness of the Gospel.

The seventeen bishops who co-signed the statement (we need not here go into the reasons for issuing the statement in the first place but it certainly had something to do with the problem of the AMRSP) give their own perception of what their role—and by extension the role of the Church as a whole, at least in the Philippines—is in the area of justice and development. And they speak of it under the rubric of political involvement. This involvement, they claim (and they are only too aware this very claim can be contested by those who disagree with their approach), is an imperative arising from the Church's primary task of preaching the Gospel.

In view of this preaching role, I believe we can take a closer look at the involvement the bishops are speaking of but now cast it in terms of role functions. We can isolate four : annunciation, denunciation, initiation, and support. Let me explain briefly what is meant by each term. In all this, I will be taking the Church to mean the institutional Church.

(*a*) *Annunciation.* Announcing the Gospel and its

message of salvation in Christ Jesus is something everyone will accept as the main mission of the Church. But this Gospel must be preached in its entirety, and in its entirety it has profound implications for all aspects of human living—political, economic, social, cultural, etc.—not simply for what we tend to narrowly define as the spiritual part of man, his soul. Hence we speak of total human development, of integral evangelisation, of full liberation—rich concepts all and interlocking. We have no trouble accepting them on an intellectual level. But speaking them out in all their fullness, in all their power? We get letters from Rome.

(*b*) *Denunciation.* The function of denouncing acts and ideas that militate against the development of peoples in accordance with Gospel principles is something we tend to consign to vinegar-tongued prophets of the Savanarola type. (We also burn them at the stake figuratively and not too figuratively.) Yet it is a task that is as necessary as the one of announcing. These two tasks complement each other. Denunciation is something that comes hard to us Southeast Asians—for cultural reasons: direct confrontation is alien to most of us; the indirect approach is our way, so we are told. True enough. But just as true is the constant need, as long as we are sinners, of the task of denouncing. Somehow we have not yet learnt to denounce—indirectly.

(*c*) *Initiation.* Initiating action for justice and development is probably the hardest—and the fuzziest—of the role functions we are discussing here. The stock objection to the Church's entry into this kind of action is that the areas of politics and economics, the hubs around which developmental problems revolve, are the layman's proper spheres, not the cleric's; and the principle of subsidiarity must be strictly followed in this instance. The problem is that we can come up with all sorts of distinctions and sub-distinctions about lay and clerical roles, but when we are faced with the concrete realities of, for instance, paralysing fear, seemingly hopeless structures, institutionalised injustice and oppression—and of people in the grips of all these—what do we do? Especially in a socio-cultural situation, such as ours is, where the Church is looked up to, is expected to lead? For the moment our approach has been quite pragmatic : *solvitur ambulando.* The need of the moment is to initiate action because nobody else does. So we act. We believe that is rationale enough—and it is deeply Gospel. But, of course, there are cardinals who say with the state : 'It *ain't* so'.

(*d*) *Support.* Where initiatives for justice and development are already being taken, defining the Church's role in terms of support is easy enough. But what I have in mind here is not just any kind of supportive action but *programmatic* : action that is well-thought out and planned, for the execution of which the Church is willing to stick her neck out, at the disposal of which she is willing to put her resources in genuine Gospel service. Are we capable of this kind of support? Those who try to give it, strangely, are immediately tagged Communists—both within and without the Church.

There probably are other functions. And certainly there are other ways of looking at the Church's role. Also, the four functions discussed above may not be distinct at all. But whatever addition or subtraction, denial or modification, is to be made about these basic ideas, any Church role-definition must include people-action. In talking of the four functions above, we limited ourselves to the role of the Church as institution. And the impression may have been given that in our scheme of things people are the *objects* of evangelisation, of liberation and development. Not at all. People are and must be the *subjects* of all we have been talking about here: they too must announce, they too must denounce, initiate, support; they too must preach the Gospel, witness to the Gospel. I think this is what Church as people means.

Hence the importance of first defining what Church is all about. For only if we have an idea—a working definition—of who we are, what we are, will we be able to ask what we can do, what we can give—and why. The seventeen bishops who wrote the statement I quoted from earlier were most conscious of this fact and they started out with the very general notion of Church as People of God. What does it really mean?

I do not know, except in a very general way, what today's theologians are evolving in the area of ecclesiology. But those of us in pastoral work—and pastoral work among impoverished masses of people—do propose that any definition of the Church, at least among people labouring under crushing poverty, must take cognisance of these elements :*

(*a*) a concern for and an involvement in the problems and affairs of men;

---

* Taken in slightly modified form from the author's article on 'The Church Government and Development', *Impact,* April 1976, p. 134.

(*b*) a positive sharing in their struggles to achieve their hopes and aspirations for a full human life;

(*c*) a view of man as a total being in whom physical needs are not merely something to be tolerated in the light of what is narrowly conceived as his spiritual needs; hence

(*d*) a concept of salvation which takes in human existence in all its aspects and involves it fully in the process of metanoia; and, finally,

(*e*) a preaching that reaches into the very depths of man's humanity and challenges him to live the Gospel in a total, integrated way, no matter what the external and internal constraints are to such a living. In short, Church is people attempting to live the mystery of the Risen Lord with all its implications for everything that is human; it is not merely a set of static relationships which we call the institutional Church.

## Towards the New Creation

I would like to end this discussion by returning to the idea we started with: the *global village*. I believe it is a very Christian concept, and while the term has been used earlier to put in sharp contrast the differences between two great worlds of development, it can also be used as the one unitive concept that can and must give meaning to any development scheme in any country, no matter what the level of (economic) development. For the global village is indeed a new creation and towards this new creation the Church has plenty to contribute.

That contribution, specific to the Church—I can only think of it in terms of a *vision*. It is a vision that springs from the Gospel and keeps returning to the Gospel for clearer and clearer focusing; yet also a vision that must be discovered by every generation, in each local Church, and worked out according to their special genius as a people. It is a vision that must lead to action by people, for people, with people, a vision to be realised and elaborated further in life, ever evolving into a more and more genuine incarnation of Christ in history.

In the final analysis, is this what our 'involvement' is all about? And is it the only corrective of the myopic selfishness that we noted earlier is general among most peoples today? If so, we as Church are failing somewhere.

# 3.
# Proclaiming Liberty to Captives
# II: The Liberty of Captives

FRANCISCO F. CLAVER, S.J.

*Ideologies and Ideologues*

It is a strange fact—and it bothers us no end—that committed Christians in many countries of Southeast Asia who take the social teachings of the Church at face value and, more significantly, try to act on them, are immediately pilloried as Communists or Communist sympathisers. Often by Churchmen too. It is a sad pass we are in. We can worry about relatively piddling things like clerical garb, Communion in the hands, correct liturgical vestments and gestures, and other such minutiae, but not about unjust wages, government by decree, farcical referendums, lack of due process, torture of prisoners, events that affect people's lives most intensely. Or, we may worry about these but without concerning ourselves with them to the point of acting. This lack of wit between what we say are our concerns as Church and what we do about those concerns forces many a real Christian to join the rebels in the hills. And we wonder why. And wondering, we come up with solutions such as: more dialogue with Communists (so long as we do not get caught talking with them!), more analysis of their methods, more research into their mentality. But we avoid radical solutions like doing something about the social conditions on which Communism thrives.

We ended Part I by noting very briefly that the Church's main contribution to the making of a better world and the attainment of justice and peace could well lie in providing men with a vision that comes from the Gospel. The suggestion was vague, I admit, couched in very general terms. Can we specify this vision more concretely, bring it down to a level of description and discourse that directly lends itself to *praxis*? I do not know if we can. I only know we should. However, as was suggested, this vision must be worked out anew by each generation, by each people. It is perhaps best then to delineate, not a particular form of the Gospel vision, but the process—or at least some ingredients in the process—of arriving at a *common* vision. I stress the word 'common', because if this vision we speak of is to be effective, it must be *shared*, at least by the people of a local Church.

It is this fact that makes me rather wary of ideologies and ideologues. The underlying premises of this bias (it is admittedly a bias) should become clearer in what follows. I would like simply to note here that we have not bothered to make the 'proper' distinctions between development and liberation, for instance, or to opt for one ideology over another (e.g. socialism over capitalism). This may seem surpassing strange in view of our insistence on the need of a vision, of programmatic action, of people-involvement.

Paradoxically, this is the very reason I say I am wary of ideologies and their champions. For an ideology is a particular vision, a particular programme of action, a particular way of people-involvement. I do not quarrel with the fact of ideology itself, with the need of ideology. But I quarrel with the *usual* manner in which ideological visions are forced/shared. Hence our concern with process.

## The Attitudes of Liberty

Let me begin by setting forth briefly what I believe should be basic attitudes on the part of the Church— the official Church, principally—in the fulfilment of her role vis-à-vis development and liberation. Since our main theme is liberation theology, let us call these 'the attitudes of liberty'. There is more to them than mere nomenclature. I will deal with only two: the attitude of trust and the attitude of learning, simple enough ideas but quite upsetting, I am afraid, for many a current mind-set.

(*a*) *Trust.* The Church must begin to trust people, to really believe in *their* basic good sense. I do not by any means limit this 'good sense' to practical matters, to areas which we readily (or should I say grudgingly?) concede are theirs by role and competence. I also include the once sacrosanct fields of ecclesiastical elites—theologians and philosophers, spiritual writers and—yes—even canon lawyers. For too long we have provided all the answers for the people, we have done all the thinking for them. It is time they begin to come up with answers of their own, to think on their own. The People of God are not a blank mass, unthinking, uncritical, unable to grasp, let alone deal with, the more abstruse points, say, of high theologising. They are not theologians, true, certainly not of the type who staff the Holy Office. But

neither are they so prone to heresy and error (as we seem
to like to think) without our enlightened guidance. They
do have some answers of their own. The problem is:
Can we trust them? Can we accept their answers? Can
we learn from them?

(b) *Learning.*  This brings us to our other attitude—
the attitude of learning. The Church that trusts should,
by that very fact, be also a Church that learns. From the
people, that is. It seems we have stressed too much in the
past our teaching role: only *we* can safeguard purity of
doctrine, only *we* can untangle and interpret for our
people the fine subtleties of doctrinal orthodoxy? I
wonder. It seems we have forgotten that complementary
to teaching is learning—even for the Holy, Roman,
Catholic Church.

The Bishops of Asia, meeting in April 1974, spoke of
a 'dialogue of life' with their respective peoples. If they
are serious about this dialogue, the most elementary interpretation I would give their words is this: that they are
open to the possibility of being taught by the people; that
they believe there are insights into life, gleaned from the
people's profound ancestral wisdom; that they can learn
from them a richer interpretation of the Gospel. This
requires great depths of humility from us, teachers of the
truth; and genuine faith too that the Spirit does indeed
breathe not only in the hierarchy but in the people as
well.

In this connection I often wonder what we, and the
theologians among us especially, mean when we say
that the *sensus fidelium* is a valid *locus theologicus*. I fear
we give this *locus* the lowest place in our catalogue of
theological proofs. Is it not time to give it the pride of

place it deserves? For I firmly believe this *sensus*—I equate it with that basic good sense I spoke of earlier but now fully suffused with faith—has much to do with the fashioning of the vision we are talking about here.

To give a concrete example by way of illustration of the above: as in many dioceses in the southern part of the Philippines, we have been pushing hard for the development of lay leaders to be the catalysts in our work of fostering basic Christian communities. These men—depending on the *trust* their respective pastors are ready to give them—perform tasks in their communities (centred on the village chapel): baptising, preaching, distributing Communion, conducting services of the word on Sundays, etc., tasks that used to be the sole prerogatives of the priest. But in addition to these, they also perform less 'churchy' functions in the community in the general attempt to integrate life and faith in a more intimate manner than tradition has allowed us to do so far.

Two months ago our lay leaders met for a whole day's evaluation of their efforts on a diocesan-wide level. (This is part of their on-going programme of training.) I sat in on some of their sessions. What I witnessed was not exactly unexpected, but I never fail to marvel, none the less, at the quality and depth of thinking that goes on among people that theological manuals (of an age past, I hope) used to refer to as *rudes*. These lay leaders were mostly men of the soil, farming folk, hardened with toil, poor. They were considering recent happenings connected with martial law government and issues raised by those very happenings, more specifically, the issues of freedom of conscience and the use of violence. I came away deeply

impressed. Those farmers were able to discuss by themselves the fine nuances of the principle of double effect,
of the lesser evil, other subtle points of moral theology,
and more importantly, apply them to their own life-
situation and come up with proposals for a line of action
that did imply some vision of how faith and life should
interpenetrate. The kind of discerning they did, I
thought, would have been worthy of more professedly
intellectual milieus like yours in this conference.

Perhaps I idealise too much. But the incident I cite
is by no means an isolated experience. It is the repeated
experience of many of my priests and religious who work
closely with the people at the grassroots level—and allow
themselves to learn from the latter. Mao's constantly
reiterated injunction to 'learn from the people' is something they have practised as a matter of course. And
this probably is the reason they are often dismissed as
crypto-Maoists. But whether of Maoist origin or not, this
trust in the people and this learning from them are most
necessary in the process of arriving at a Gospel-inspired
vision—in fact are part of the vision itself.

## *The Praxis of Liberty*

There are a number of operative concepts that are
of importance in the task of vision-formation. I will limit
myself to only three, all from Vatican II : *participation,
dialogue, co-responsibility*. For the past half-decade or
so, we in Mindanao-Sulu, the southernmost section of the
Philippines, have been quite obsessed with these ideas.
The obsession has worked wonders in the churches of
the region. It has also created problems. The explanation
is not hard to come by : these ideas contain in them-

selves dynamisms which are simply waiting to be released, dynamisms that mean much for fuller human living, hence necessarily problematic. But if they create problems too, sometimes of great magnitude, strangely these same problems have a way of becoming answers to the very questions and difficulties they pose.

(*a*) *Participation.* The principle of participation, simply stated, means that people must have a share in the forming of decisions that in any way touch their well-being, both as individuals and as community. Self-help, self-activity, self-organisation—these are all implied in the term, as is also goal-setting. The rationale for this is simply stated too : the more people share in the process of decision-making that leads to common action, the firmer the support for the decision taken, the deeper the commitment to its execution. This principle is quite fundamental in the literature on social change. And we have no trouble accepting its necessity in the 'secular' process of development. Somehow we are not too accepting of it—Vatican notwithstanding—in the area of Church life. For among other things it calls into question the traditional role-structuring within the Church of bishops, priests, religious, laity. Or perhaps it is not so much a matter of questioning as of redefining roles—and putting life and reality into them as redefined.

(*b*) *Dialogue.* The redefinition we have in mind can only take place meaningfully in a Church-in-dialogue— and this brings us to our second principle. We throw the word 'dialogue' around quite a bit, but I doubt whether much real dialogue takes place. If it did, the often deep polarisations we find among people, both within and without the Church, would not be so common. For by dialogue we mean people coming together, reasoning together, listening, and willing to learn from the listening, open to the possibility of new insights and influences from those they are in dialogue with. I feel that the polarisations we have in the Church today do not come from splits between conservative and liberal elements so much as from any two factions of closed-minded people, whether conservatives or liberals, who cannot, will not learn from one another. Give me conservatives and liberals who are both open-minded, in real dialogue with one another, and I can guarantee you a living Church, deeply divided at times, perhaps, but never frustratingly polarised.

From the sheerly sociological point of view, dialogue is all of a piece with the idea of participation, and their common note is *sharing*. It also denotes consensus—a prerequisite for any genuine community, especially of a pluralist nature—but a consensus that itself is open to further evolution, as circumstances change, as new data are brought in or new perceptions developed.

(c) *Co-responsibility.* Basic to the process of sharing that is participation and dialogue is the principle of shared responsibility. People coming to a consensus, deciding on a communal act, must take responsibility for the life of their community, for the directions they choose to follow as a community. Again, it is all most common-sensical, something that people in 'primitive' communities all over the world do as a matter of day-to-day living, accept as basic to their whole interaction in community.

Applying this principle closer to home—if we accept it as operational in the Church, that is—I cannot help wondering if we are willing to extend it to all areas of Church life, to test it as a real operative principle of life and thought in the Church. I am afraid it will never be really operative as long as we remain mistrustful of the capability of the rank-and-file Church to be truly responsible. For basic to the effective assuming of responsibility in any human society is a minimum of mutual trust among interacting members. We see the need for this kind of responsibility in the Church. We talk about it. But it will never be shared unless those who presently have a monopoly of it begin to actually share it. It is as simple as that.

## Church as Communication

We adverted briefly above to the fact that great, sometimes immense, problems arise when we try making the principles of participation, dialogue and co-responsibility really work. All sorts of questions arise: What is the bishop's role in decision-making processes in the diocese, or the pastor's in the parish? Who is to judge when a communal decision springs from a false interpretation of the Gospel? Who has the final responsibility in all this?

These are valid questions. And they cannot be set aside by simply answering that these are reactions from an embattled Church: that participation would be against authoritarianism; dialogue against dogmatism; co-responsibility against paternalism—all three 'isms' the actually dominant principles of government and thought within the hierarchical Church. Rather than get involved in what could be futile discussions of the pros and cons of these broad generalisations, it would seem more profitable to take a brief look at what could be an opening to the possibility of arriving at some answers to these questions.

I suggest we return to our notion of the Church. With all the talk about models and structures, it will do no harm to propose one more : the Church as Communication. Indeed this in no way differs from the concept of Church as People of God, but there are a number of points that, I feel, may be brought out better from the viewpoint of communication.

(*a*) *Creating Forums.*   We hardly talk about public opinion in the Church (although the *sensus fidelium* is in essence a form of such an opinion). Or if we do, we rarely think in terms of its on-going formation, of its fostering and evolvement. Actually we do, in a way : schools, mass media, encyclicals, pastoral letters, the pulpit—these are all geared towards forming Church opinion conformed and conformable to the Gospel. This is all right as far as the *teaching* Church is concerned. But what about the *learning* Church ? Communication is a two-way street. Hence there must be the possibility of *feedback*, of response to communication. This is what is largely missing.

Hence the need of creating forums, at all levels and among every sector of Church membership—forums that are working vehicles of communication which make it possible for people to speak up and be listened to and be taken seriously. Vatican II was cognisant of the need. Thus the instituting of Bishops' Synods, Priests' Senates, Diocesan Pastoral Councils, Parish Councils, Church groups of all kinds. But in practice these involved mainly traditional Church leaders (both clerical and lay). Many of these forums have been created, but whether they are functioning or not *as* forums is another question. The need is to make them genuinely do so. And for this it is necessary to make the elemental unit of communication within the Church the basic Christian community.

(*b*) *Focus on People.* If these communities are to become the basic units of communication, their focus will have to be the common good of the people as community, as Church : their life, their concerns, their problems. In this focusing we will include all we have said earlier about the elements that must go into a working ecclesiology, about the role-functions of the Church but now as people of God and not merely as institution. And this focus will itself be the starting point of the process of the people's coming to a vision of their common task in the Gospel.

In all the above we have bypassed a question that the canonically-minded insist on asking : What is the nature of these forums we speak of ? At some point they will have to become decision-making bodies; if so, will they be consultative or deliberative in nature ? This question, I know full well, is being asked of the Synod of Bishops itself, of lesser other conferences and councils in the Church. The trouble is that when it is asked and canonical answers are given, we usually end up with *paper* synods, pastoral councils and the like. This makes me think it is the wrong question to ask—at least at this time. If we are convinced that these forums are vital to the life of the Church at this point in history, it may well be premature trying to articulate—and hence to constrict —that life in the vocabulary and limitations of a legal system that was not made for it.

At any rate, I believe we can transcend the problem

if we make these forums really focus themselves on people, on people-problems, on people-concerns. For when real communication takes place at this level of interest, decision-making follows most naturally. And the problem of competence and authority somehow solves itself.

(c) *Self-Regulating Mechanisms.*    This is by no means to opt for unrestricted freedom in the Church. Although life concerns are wide and far-ranging, there are necessarily limits to them. Any community of men and women engaged in constant dialogic interaction will discover those limits for themselves and will act ordinarily within those same limits. This interaction, participative, dialogic, co-responsible, will itself be the mechanism that will enable the community to regulate itself. This capacity for self-regulation—call it the 'collective will' if you wish—is something that I would include for acceptance in the attitude of trust that was mentioned earlier.

However, we do not preclude, by any means, the possibility of the community's committing mistakes. But by the same token, we do not preclude the possibility of its correcting them when they are committed. Community consensus can go far wrong at any given moment. But in progressing (or retrograding) from consensus to consensus, the community is always aware of just where it is. It may not be always aware of all the implications of its consensus at any given time (who is, except God?), but there is always the possibility of growing in that awareness. And of changing direction from a heightened awareness.

(d) *The Discerning Community.*    What in effect we have been talking about here then is the creating of *discerning communities*: communities of people who come together to talk of their problems, to seek solutions for them, to act in concert when the need for concerted action is indicated; reflecting communities, hence self-aware; likewise self-regulating and self-contained; yet for all that, outward-looking, concerned not only with themselves but with other communities, other people. And above all, being and acting because of the Gospel, in the light of the Gospel. If such a community is the minimal unit of the universal community that we call the Church, it is also that of the even wider community that we initially called the global village. And it is its own particular grasp of the Gospel-vision that it will contribute to the building up of the latter.

As we indicated above, the Church as communication is in reality simply another version of the People of God model. If there is anything special to it, it is its incorporation into its inner design of rich insights into the nature of communication processes from cybernetics, communications and general systems theory and the like, all fertile areas of modern scientific researching. It is a measure of the Church's general acceptance of some of the points we have been talking of here that it has allowed itself, consciously I think, to be influenced by advances in the sciences, the social sciences especially. It has always been in reality a *learning* Church, but in its dogmatising, the fact tends to be forgotten—or, perhaps, not often publicly acknowledged?

There are other aspects of the Church as communication that should be further elaborated—especially the fact that the Church is in its innermost being *communication*. We leave that elaboration to professional theologians. I would only make one point here apropros of this fact: the more *internal* communication takes place within the Church, the more faithfully and convincingly it will speak out the Message of the Word. The converse is also true, of course.

## Development and Liberation

I would like to conclude by returning to our main theme of development and liberation. We may seem to have strayed far from it by bringing into the orbit of our consideration what seem like too many extraneous topics. Not really. The fact is, since our concentration is on the role of the Church in development and liberation, and we have defined this role in terms of vision-formation, a process, we have had to go into certain key ideas in that process. Hence the stress on the twin attitudes of trust and learning, on the acting principles of participation, dialogue, and co-responsibility, and finally on the Church itself as communication. That process, when one comes down to it, is itself *the* process of development and liberation.

(a) *Captives and Liberators.* For the very process of elaborating *together* a vision in the Gospel, communicating it within and outside the community, and, more importantly, striving to realise it in action, in concert with others, *in* and *as* community, is development of peoples in a most profound and real sense. It is also liberation in an equally profound and real sense. For it is people, thinking together, responding together, acting together, who must be the agents and architects of their own individual and collective good. It is they, the *captives* in all manner of oppressive situations, who must work out their own liberty. Ideologues will come and go, prophets and kings and priests too, for that matter, all with their own modes and models of developing and liberating *others*, all with their own special visions *for* others. They all will pass away from the scene as just so many loud words, no more, no less, unless they themselves become part of the 'others'. Then only will they begin to speak a liberating message.

This is the reason for that wariness with ideologies I referred to earlier. Their liberating vision is all too often obfuscated—even denied—in the rigidly dogmatic manner in which they are presented as the only answers to a given situation. In the discerning community scheme of things, ideas and programmes of action, even mystiques and ideologies, must be subject to scrutiny, open to modification and change, responsive to realities as people see them at any given moment. The individual genius of the ideologue must be critically examined by the collective genius of the people, and together they must arrive at a common—if momentary—vision of their liberation and development, for both captives and liberators are involved in this process.

*(b) Responsiveness.* The emphasis in all this is on responsiveness. And this in turn calls for adaptability, flexibility, even in such a holy institution as the Church. In the final analysis, the acid test of any definition we reach in regard to Church roles and functions in the struggle for man's development and liberation is whether it does or does not carry the note of responsiveness to the deepest aspirations of people in the here and now, to their realities, to their conditions, to their lives in the flesh-and-blood present.

One final observation. Our perspective in all this—at

C

least so I would like to think—has been a pastoral one. This is not in any way to condone whatever sins or heresies I may have here been guilty of, but to state a simple yet most important fact. True enough, many sins are committed in the name of pastoral concern and action. But as we noted somewhere above, those very sins could well be our salvation. That is cryptic enough, I think. Let me end with it to keep up the image of 'oriental inscrutability'.

# 4.
# Political Structures and Personal Development

## GARRET FITZGERALD

The passions for domination and acquisition—dominating other people and acquiring material possessions—are striking characteristics of the human race. The former no doubt owes much to man's animal origins but the latter is more specifically human—and is a feature of civilised man in settled society. This means that it is of relatively recent origin, for no more than 300 generations have elapsed since hunters first began to abandon their nomadic existence and to settle down as farmers, and later as artisans.

Taken together these two passions account for the violence and horror of so much of human history, and for the condition in which much of the human race lives today, ruled by self-appointed governments, many of whose members abuse their positions to secure for themselves and their families privileges or possessions beyond the needs of their position, and who deal with potential threats to their authority by acts of repression.

Abuses of power and the acquisition of inordinate wealth are not, however, confined to members of self-appointed governments and their entourages. The structure of our societies, whether they be capitalistic or communist, are such that gross inequalities of wealth extend far beyond the purely political sphere. This is most marked in capitalist-type societies, but is present in communist regimes too.

The instincts to dominate and to acquire do not, however, represent the totality of human nature. There is a higher side to humanity, morally and aesthetically. Moreover, the instinct to dominate is matched by a will to freedom, and that of acquisition by a will to secure an equitable spread of material wealth, so that none need starve, or freeze, or suffer deprivation. And beyond these, there is the instinct to raise man above the level of his lowest instincts, to create types of society in which good rather than evil will be likely to prevail, and to make it possible for every human being to secure the fullest development of his moral personality, his intellectual capacity and his aesthetic endowment. This is the instinct to liberation.

Liberation is not a simple concept, however, because it involves both a negative reaction against two quite different baser instincts—domination and acquisitiveness—and also a positive will to secure human development. Three somewhat different concepts of liberation have thus emerged—the concepts of political freedom, of equality, and of personal development. And because of the attraction of simple concepts, and the single-mindedness with which human beings pursue their aims, whether for evil or for good, those who contest the evils of domination and those who contest the evils of acquisitiveness each tend to ignore the other problem, and to have an incomplete vision of a balanced human society.

The *liberal* directs his attention against tyranny in all

its forms, and is sometimes oblivious of the fact that the mere absence of tyranny is insufficient to guarantee to human beings a fair share of material resources, or the possibility of personal development. Many democratic societies are shot through with economic injustice—for the right of universal suffrage in a pluralist democracy offers no guarantee of social justice. This is because those who are most under-privileged are also those who least know how to exercise their franchise to secure a betterment of their condition. And those who are the 'haves' in such societies know all too well how to organise themselves in defence of their interests, and to offer suport to, or withdraw support from, politicians in the manner most likely to secure a perpetuation of their material advantages.

The insensitivity of some liberals to economic justice in democratic societies is more than matched by the insensitivity of some socialists to individual freedom. Some *socialists* believe indeed that individual freedom is incompatible with economic justice—and point to the economic injustices prevalent in pluralist democracies as evidence in support of their theses. Others believe merely that personal freedom must take second place, in priority and in time, to the achievement of economic justice. Either way their view is an incomplete one, deriving from a simplistic view of an inherently complex problem —the problem of *balancing* freedom and economic justice, which may indeed be in a state of inherent tension vis-à-vis each other, but neither of which can be written off in favour of the other without creating a society that will be incompletely human.

Liberals and socialists are both in a sense reactionaries,

however—they are reacting in one case against the evil
of domination and in the other against the evil of acquisitiveness. Their views of society are not merely incomplete,
but are in a sense negative, because directed *against* particular evils. It is because these two philosophies, at any
rate in their most pure forms, are each incomplete and
largely negative in inspiration that many people have
increasingly turned to a more positive view of the human
problem—to the concept of the personal development of
man in society as the crucial issue. This concept sub-
sumes both the liberal and socialist views—for full
human development could not exist without the freedom
to choose how society is to be organised and by whom
it is to be guided, nor without a distribution of material
resources that will not merely guarantee all against
hunger and cold and other deprivation, but will provide
each human being with the means of fulfilling himself
morally, intellectually and aesthetically.

What political structures are best attuned to the
achievement of human development? At this stage in
human society any answer to this question has to be
somewhat tentative, despite the vast experience of different political systems in many lands over many millennia.
We can, however, observe how certain existing political
systems aid or inhibit human development, and we can
consider what problems might arise if we sought to
develop a political system more specifically adapted to
the task of human development.

First, it is clear that all existing political systems are
very imperfect means of securing the end of individual
fulfilment for all members of society. The pluralist democratic system as we have developed it has a number of

obvious merits in this respect, but falls very far short of
the ideal. Amongst its principal merits is that it is better
adapted than any other system of which we have experience to inhibit tyranny and gross corruption by rulers.
The ready availability of alternative governmental teams
who can be substituted, one for the other, through the
ballot box rather than by riot or revolution, keeps a rein
on the over-ambitious and on those who would abuse
power for personal advantage.

Of course the system is not perfect even for these purposes, but it is better than any other in this respect. That
it is still defective even in controlling personal ambition
or acquisitiveness amongst rulers reflects in part at least
a certain insensitivity to such evils amongst the electorate;
some voters prefer rulers who fall short of the highest
standards in these respects, but whom they judge to be
more effective and tougher politicians, to people of
higher integrity but, in such voters' view, of lesser
effectiveness. This is a source of danger in the pluralist
democratic system, of which all should be conscious.

Those concerned with the moral health of society,
whether they be clerical or lay moralists, could usefully
direct attention to this aspect of politics. Separation of
Church and State, desirable as it is for the sake of both,
does not mean that inadequate standards in politics—
any more than in the Church!—should be exempt from
critical comment—which, however, to be effective must
be informed and balanced comment. It is fair to add that
in Ireland we have been very largely spared the excesses
of political ambition and the debasement of corruption
which are features of many other democratic systems. We
have our own defects, however, which too rarely arouse

critical comment, including the generally accepted practice of permitting political considerations to influence
decisions in the narrow range of appointments that are ex-
cluded from the impartial system of public competition.

At the same time one must recognise an opposite—
and indeed much greater—danger that an exaggerated
view of the prevalence of defects of this kind in a democratic political system, and of the inevitable selectiveness
with which political parties press their claims for support
at election times, may give rise to a quite unwarranted
cynicism about democratic politics—a cynicism highly
dangerous to the political freedom which this system
protects. Here we face a very real dilemma, which is
not generally appreciated. The essential character of
pluralist democracy lies in the element of choice that it
offers to the electorate at certain maximum intervals of
time. This choice involves competition for votes—and
this competition, however high a standard politicians
may set themselves, is bound to involve some degree of
disedification and disillusionment amongst people who
approach politics simplistically, ignoring the fact that it
is a human discipline, subject to all the defects of human
nature. The danger to pluralist democracy as a system
lies in the fact that its greatest virtues are negative ones;
that it inhibits tyranny and gross corruption; and negative virtues do not easily inspire passionate enthusiasm,
especially if they are accompanied by propaganda which
by its selectivity of exaggeration disedifies many of the
electors.

This problem is, of course, more acute where pluralist
politics is not divided on clear-cut ideological lines. In
the absence of such clear ideological divisions there is a

tendency for the electorate to dismiss the different parties as all being much-of-a-muchness, and to assume that those involved in them, not being aligned against each other along neat and easily identifiable ideological lines, must be merely 'out for themselves'.

A further problem with the pluralist democratic system is that in most countries the choice of candidates to be put before the electorate is made by fairly small groups of party activists, whose choice may sometimes be determined more by internal party considerations than by the desirability of presenting the electorate with a range of able, dedicated, and idealistic contenders for office.

Finally, there is the problem that this system of government is prone to being over-influenced by organised pressure groups. In the worst cases this may involve corrupt practices though never as gross as in many dictatorships. In most West European countries like ourselves the excessive influence of organised pressure groups derives from the fact that election results are determined by the small minority who *change* their votes, rather than by the majority who do not; and amongst this minority there will be organised groups who will threaten a withdrawal of their members' support from a party that does not advocate policies which are to the advantage of the group in question—or will offer their members' support to a party that 'toes the line' with regard to their sectional interests. Even though many of those belonging to these groups may in fact disregard the advice given them by their leaders, politicians at election times, seeking to scrape the bottom of all available barrels for votes, may be tempted to trim their sails in the direction of the more powerful and better organised groups.

D

These more powerful and better-organised groups are always amongst the 'haves' in society. The under-privileged are, almost *a priori*, under-organised. Old age pensioners, the unemployed, other socially disadvantaged groups, and indeed consumers *qua* consumers, are never organised in such a way as to be able to influence so effectively the decisions of political parties.

In so far as political parties do in fact pay considerable attention to the needs of these disadvantaged groups, often in the face of great hostility from the 'haves' in society, this reflects in large measure the idealism of politicians, and their consciousness of having the duty of representing both the general interest and the interest of weaker sections of the community in the face of the big battalions. These virtues are rarely claimed by politicians, and even more rarely recognised by others. They exist, nevertheless.

I have dwelt at some length on certain defects of the pluralist democratic system, first of all because it is the political system we have in Ireland, and secondly because if we are not conscious of these defects, and do not work assiduously to minimise and where possible to eliminate them, we may endanger the existence of this system which, I repeat, has the inestimable advantage of alone securing freedom from tyranny and from gross corruption.

At the same time, it is evident that the pluralist democratic system does not easily break down class barriers or provide anything approaching equality of opportunity for the children of different social groups. It *tends* in this direction, certainly, and has created a society in which there is a much greater measure of equality of opportunity than existed a century ago before universal suffrage was introduced and our pluralist system was thus democratised. But the process is a desperately slow one, achieving results not over years or even decades, but over periods of generations. Thus even after all the social and educational reforms of the current century, the chance of a child of a poor family in Dublin achieving the same measure of personal development—never mind earning-capacity—as a child of well-to-do parents is fractional. The class into which one is born is still by far the most powerful determinant of the opportunity for personal development in societies like ours which are pluralist democracies.

There are those who draw from this the conclusion that a socialist system of the Eastern European type is morally preferable to a pluralist democracy. They argue that the loss of certain personal freedoms—in so far as they admit their loss in these types of socialist societies— is a reasonable price to pay for the much greater possibilities for equality of opportunity which these societies are held to provide. It is not sufficient to dismiss this argument without consideration, by simply stating as an axiom that personal freedom transcends all other considerations—for such a line of argument can all too easily become an excuse for doing nothing about the defects of our type of pluralist democracy. Moreover, such an argument could in the longer run prove counter-productive—for, as we have seen happen in some countries, if a substantial section of the population is under-privileged, and is offered no prospect, even over a period of years, of securing the same opportunities for its children through the democratic political process, they may in time be led to the conclusion that only violent action will redress this evil, and that violence is justified in such a last resort.

There are some in our society who do not contest that it tends to inhibit the personal development of a high proportion of our people, but who hold that any attempt to remedy this would involve such a redistribution of income and wealth as to remove from our economic system the element of incentive which alone can make our type of predominantly capitalist mixed economy work. One can allow that it may be true that, at a given moment in time, and especially in a period of world economic recession, an attempt to move too far, too fast might weaken the existing economic structure, thus reducing growth, the expansion of resources, and the chances of remedying the injustices of our society in the future.

But to accept that this argument is true in the longer run would be to condemn our politico-economic system as inherently immoral and therefore indefensible. If our system were in fact to be incapable, even over a period of time, of evolving so as to create genuine equality of opportunity, through an erosion of the class divisions which at present fatally inhibit the achievement of this objective, then it would be hard indeed to resist the logic of socialism even in its extremer forms.

Thus it is that those who resist change in our present system constitute the greatest danger to its survival; and those who seek to move it along the path towards social justice are its best defenders. Social democrats are, and have always been seen by extreme socialists to be, the greatest danger to the type of non-democratic socialism which these extremists defend and advocate.

If I have seemed in what I have just said to link closely pluralist democracy and the predominantly capitalist mixed economy with which we are familiar, it is because the two are in fact closely linked with each other. The economic choice offered by the market system is closely linked to the political choice offered by the pluralist democratic system. The link is capable of evolution, however. I do not believe that a pluralist democracy must necessarily be a consumerist society. But only a highly educated democratic society will be able to withstand the pressures of consumerism and to control this exploitatory system. By 'highly educated' I mean a society whose members are encouraged to develop to the full their faculties of critical judgement and scepticism about conventional wisdom, and to develop their individual talents, which alone can make those concerned immune to the attempts to drug their senses in the interest of commercial gain.

Here we face a problem which we have been too willing to ignore—the problem of the relative roles of value-transmission and personality-development within an educational system. Because of a particular sociological view that has been widely held in the Roman Catholic Church, we have tended to view our educational system primarily as a means of transmitting inherited values. The denominational education system finds its justification in this view of education, carried to the point where not merely the transmission of Christian values, but of a particular set of Christian values, is seen as the appropriate determinant of the whole structure of education.

Without entering into a discussion of the merits of this thesis, which is sometimes argued—on both sides—

with more passion than scientific rigour, one must in the context of this discussion raise the question as to whether one can ultimately reconcile this view of the educational process with the fullest personal development of the individual, giving him the command over himself or herself that will make it possible to withstand the pressures towards conformity with the values of a consumer society.

Can one at the same time teach a child to accept unquestioningly a particular set of values, rarely argued from first principles, while at the same time developing in all other respects the kind of critical faculties which are necessary to withstand the pressure to conformity of so much of the modern way of life? There is a question here that we should ask ourselves honestly, and seek to answer honestly. We are certainly not entitled to assume without further ado that an educational system as strongly biased as ours is towards value-transmission is capable of, or is in fact, achieving the kind of personal development of the individual that will enable him or her to withstand pressures of the kind that are imposed on us from outside our shores.

In this connection one has to face the fact that it is in Southern European countries of the more authoritarian Roman Catholic tradition that the more extreme forms of socialism have made their greatest progress in Western Europe, whereas in Northern European countries, with their Protestant tradition of private judgement, moderate social democrat ideas have held their own. Can we in Ireland be sure that in continuing to gear our educational system primarily towards the transmission of a particular set of values, based on authority and tradition, we are not sowing dragon's teeth, preparing the ground for a too-ready acceptance by a future generation of an alternative and opposite set of ideas, based on acceptance of a different kind of authority?

At the least we ought to seek to balance the value-transmission element of our educational system by a strong emphasis on personal development and by encouragement of a critical approach to the conformism of so much of modern society—which already has such a powerful grip on the younger generation. Our system should extol above all moral courage in withstanding pressures to conformity, whether with the passing vogue of the times, with commercialised imported *mores*, or with past conventions that have no intrinsic value. Instead of resisting criticism of our institutions and our way of life, both of which contain much dross as well as much of enduring value, we should encourage the constructive element in criticism—the element that points the way to a better alternative and is not content merely with tearing down what exists.

This requires a dialogue between the generations—a willingness of those of middle or later age to confront and argue out with the young the shape that our future society should have. Instead of condemning ideas for change we should be prepared to tease out their implications with those who propound them. The unreason of authoritarianisms of right and left is exposed by rational argument; unchallenged these doctrines can develop a spurious attraction for young people, to many of whom the society we have today is not so strikingly moral or just as to demand without further argument the rejection of any alternative.

Our system of government is a representative one,

rather than a direct democracy. The reasons for this are multiple; they include the impracticability of direct democracy in societies numbering millions, or tens of millions of inhabitants; and the dangers of populism in a system where all decisions are taken by direct vote of the electorate, easily swayed by the emotions of the moment.

The virtues of representative democracy are well established, but in large and complex communities this system can remove decision-making to such a distance from the people as to alienate them from the whole process of government. We live in an age when we can see this happening all around us. Within nation-States there is a development of regionalism, which in some instances may threaten the very existence of the State. At every level there is frustration and resentment at what are regarded as the rigidities of an over-bureaucratic system. Local interests vie with each other for expression—and for the right to determine the development of their own environment. At the same time there is a movement towards industrial democracy, as workers seek some control over circumstances of their employment. And both students and teachers seek a say in the running of educational institutions in which in the past they have had to be content with being passive agents.

All this is a healthy, and one may feel, overdue assertion of human dignity. Modern society has become inhuman in its scale, in its uniformity, and in its uncontrollability as seen from the viewpoint of its ordinary members. The problem of reforming this complex mechanism so as to humanise it is one that we have only begun to face. All that we know at this stage is that it will be an extremely difficult task.

The difficulty derives from the fact that our society has become so complex that each individual is playing a number of different and often contradictory roles. He is both producer and consumer; taxpayer and tax beneficiary; he is at one and the same time a commuter seeking speedy access—often in his own private vehicle at peak periods—to his place of work, and a domestic person, resenting the intrusion of modern communications and technology on his environment. At one level he wants to be left alone, to live where he has always lived, in an unchanged environment, to be free from the burden of taxation, and to spend his own money in his own way. At another level he demands services and facilities whose provision is incompatible with the pre-existing environment, and which require vast public expenditure on health and educational services, on housing, on communications, on telephones and television, and so on. And as the societal cake becomes larger, and as the cost of it rises, the urge to have it, and to eat it, becomes more and more compelling. Man is forced by the conflict between his mutually incompatible needs to be schizophrenic, and he resents it increasingly as every year passes.

The desire to recover some element of direct control over those aspects of life which impinge most directly on people is easier to satisfy in some areas than in others. The idea of teacher and student involvement in the running of educational institutions is increasingly accepted, and is being implemented gradually in various sectors of education. Worker participation in management poses more problems—there is the vexed question of whether this should involve the creation of a supervisory board

on the German model; there is the question of the role
of trade unions in such a structure; and there are problems arising from the fact that in Ireland the concept is
relatively unfamiliar to much of domestic industry, and
could create problems in relation to foreign, and especially US firms investing here. Nevertheless the movement
towards worker participation in the management of
larger firms at least is general throughout Western
Europe, and is in fact specifically envisaged by the EEC
in its draft European Company statute, so that we may
also expect a development along these lines here in the
years ahead.

There is, however, the more general problem of securing a more direct involvement of people in the political
process that determines the pattern of the society in
which they live. At present the level of involvement in
this process is small. Something like six per cent of the
adult population claim to belong to a political party,
though in many cases their involvement is peripheral;
and they are largely inactive save at election times. Moreover at the other end of the spectrum a large minority
of the population is clearly uninterested in the political
process, which is seen by this group as something alien
to them.

Now it may well be true that some of those who are
uninterested in politics in a pluralist democratic system
are alienated by the political party structure and by the
competition between parties for electoral support. But
it is equally true that many people become interested in
politics only because this party structure exists, providing
a framework for useful and idealistic social activity. The
problem of alienation from politics is not in fact one

peculiar to the pluralist democratic system, but reflects a very widespread passivity on the part of people with respect to the management of the society in which they live. We are all familiar with this phenomenon in vocational or local groups—with the fact that most people are content to leave the work of organisation to an active minority, except, perhaps, when some crisis arises; then a much bigger proportion than normal of those concerned assert themselves and demand direct say in handling the problem facing them.

A healthy society is organised so as to encourage a sense of involvement—starting in the schools. We have a good deal to learn in this respect. In Irish society there is a paternalist element that discourages individual and local initiative.

At the same time we must not exaggerate the possibilities of mass involvement in the running of society at all its levels. At this stage of human development at any rate, many people are prone to manipulation by skilful demagogy and relatively few are prepared for the responsibilities of sharing in the running of affairs at local or vocational level. The dangers of mass or direct democracy in these circumstances are considerable.

There is moreover a more general problem about devolution of governmental authority that we have not fully faced. Much of the work of government is strictly executive in character—it involves decisions about the allocation of resources and the provision of facilities—decisions that can be taken only by an executive body. Such matters are not capable of popular decision—because the choices are multiple; there are almost endless different ways in which public expenditure can be

allocated. Direct democracy can decide yes/no issues—
as our electorate have done on a number of occasions
at referenda—when the choice is between accepting or
rejecting a particular proposal. But direct democracy
cannot make multiple choices, such as are involved in
resource allocation. Such choices have to be delegated
to groups of people, whose decisions are then subject to
the sanction of subsequent general approval or dis-
approval, when the time comes for the public to decide
whether to keep them in office or choose a different
team to make these choices on their behalf.

There are strict limits, therefore, on the extent to
which individuals in society can join directly in taking
decisions on matters affecting their lives. What is certainly
true is that we have not reached or even approached
these limits. Our governmental system remains broadly
speaking the same as that which we inherited from a
semi-colonial type regime, which had a strong instinct
in favour of centralisation of decision-making. We have
less local democracy than most of our neighbours in
Western Europe—none of whom have yet gone to the
limit in this regard.

It is easy enough to identify this defect, and to see
that it ought to be remedied, within the limits of the
possible. It is much more difficult to do this in practice,
especially in a country suffering from chronic problems
of under-development, which are greatly aggravated by
the ready comparisons available to our people with
better-off countries nearby—some with material living
standards almost two-and-a-half times ours. Successive
governments seeking to cope with this problem, on which
has been superimposed in recent years both the problem

of security and that of the crisis in Northern Ireland, as well as the problem of adjustment to membership of the European Community, have not been able to give the necessary time to considering how our society needs to be re-structured to give its members a fuller say in the decisions that affect their lives. The difficulty of facing these multiple issues has not been eased by the traditional small size of the governmental team in Ireland.

At the same time, although we have a particular problem because of the small scale of our population and of the government machine, we also have, by virtue of the smallness of the scale of our society, an opportunity to do things that could not be attempted in mass societies comprising fifty or sixty million people. The *intimacy* of our society is a potential strength when one is attempting to achieve social cohesion through a more participatory system of government.

I have deliberately approached this question of Political Structures and Personal Development from an Irish angle—basing myself on the kind of society that we have in Ireland, and the kind of problems that we face in improving its quality. I know that the concept of liberation theology derives from another part of the world where the problems of society are very different from here. I know that in many countries in Latin America, for example, a major problem in the way of any kind of social reform is external economic exploitation, and corrupt national governments, closely linked to the economic forces which are exploiting the peoples of the countries concerned. The solutions required to problems of that kind are inevitably different from those appropriate in our society, which, despite its under-development, is a *relatively* equal partner in an inter-dependent community of States. There are, of course, those in our society who seek to propound an analogy between our circumstances and those of certain Latin American or other developing countries, but the irrelevance of the analogy is so evident that I have not felt it necessary to spend time on rebutting it. What we should be concerned with is the real defects of our society, as it exists. These are numerous enough, and serious enough, to make us think seriously about our political system, without being distracted by false comparisons.

My thesis is quite simply that the virtues of the plural-ist democratic system which we possess are important enough to merit preservation, but that this cannot and should not lead to the conclusion that our system is at present structured in a way that provides adequate oppor-tunities for human development. If, indeed, we were so complacent as to draw this conclusion, we should thereby endanger the very elements of our system that are worth preserving. The need is rather for a debate on how the system of representative democracy that we possess can be organised so as to secure the fullest oppor-tunity for human development, through the educational system, in the work-place, and in the organisation and running of local affairs. We have to face the fact that it will not be easy to organise such a debate so long as we are facing inflation and unemployment on their present scale, the threat of violence, and uncertainty about the future of Northern Ireland. We can, however, begin to prepare now for this debate which, hopefully, will prove to be a major issue of the 1980s. The publica-tion of these papers is a first step in this preparation.

# 5.
# An Irish Theology of Liberation?

ENDA MCDONAGH

## Introduction

Before discussing the substantive question it is necessary to raise the preliminary one. Can one speak of an Irish theology at all? Inevitably, it is coloured by the cultural background, but is there anything distinctive about it? An Irish theology that grows out of the Irish situation? I doubt that we have anything of that kind of any great significance. This would have been true of Latin America ten years ago, of the Philippines three or four years ago. So our lack is not necessarily a reason for being depressed or for ignoring the challenge that these countries offer us. But we have always had, and perhaps more importantly, the implicit theology of a living Christian community. 'Implicit theology' is, I realise, almost a contradiction in terms—it suggests the pre-reflective stage, and theology takes place at the reflective stage. We need to get to the reflective stage much more in the Irish situation.

There exists a considerable attraction for Irish people to adopt some models of theology developed elsewhere. This is what we have been doing. Up to Vatican II we adopted the models of the Roman schools of theology. In the wake of Vatican II we have been adopting the central European schools of theology. In some sense this is a form of theological colonisation. In some sense the Irish Theological Association has almost been a parallel with the Industrial Development Authority, where we sought theological capital abroad and tried to invest it at home. We sometimes think of ourselves as a formerly colonised and marginal country exploited now by the multi-national corporations. There would seem to be certain parallels with third world countries, and not only in the socio-economic and political spheres, but also in the theological sphere. The Latin Americans may inspire us to overcome such dependence.

## A Theology Based on the Historical Situation

What the Latin Americans stress is what happens when they are doing theology, and we have much to learn from them. One of the Latin Americans makes the point that their great advantage was that they had no native philosophy. They substituted an analysis of the social situation and their critical reflection on this in the light of faith. It would again be a mistake to take over their model uncritically. But they have a lesson that we do need a theology which is in fact a critical reflection on the basis of the historical process of the people with whom we are dealing, whether you call that liberation, or development or transformation. There is a historical development and a historical people in process to whom we belong, to whose service we are called, and it is on that people in that historical process that we ought to be reflecting in the light of our faith.

My experiment then with an 'Irish Theology of Liberation' will confine itself almost entirely to using this historical consciousness, so developed among the Latin Americans, to explore in faith some aspects of the Irish situation. Some other facets of their theology and the challenge they pose I have dealt with earlier.

## The Exploration of the Irish Historical Consciousness

It is a theological task for a number of reasons, particularly if, paradoxically, it embodies the anthropological task of understanding the man of faith who is a historical being. I am not saying this in the sense that he goes through history. We have not yet come to grips with the sheer historicity of man, the temporal character of his being. It is communal, a historical process within a community, and of course it is not a community that flows above the ground but one that has its roots firmly in the soil. So that the Irish believer is from that point of view earthy, cosmic, social, in process, in movement. And that is the person we are talking about when we are talking about the man of faith. And it is in that cosmos and movement of history, that his faith is his faith. So we must come to terms with the historical, social, cosmic process if we want to understand where and how he encounters God. It is therefore for that basic reason that I see theology as a critical reflection on the actual condition of man seen from these three points of view.

## Subject or Object of History

In this process of being a cosmic, social and historical being a man can be an object or a subject. *It is that element of object in him and that call to be subject in him that I see as at the core of understanding faith.* There is no way in which man the object can recognise and respond to God. Only man the subject can do this. If he is therefore simply the object of cosmic and historical forces he is thereby cut off from that inter-subjective relationship we call faith. It is in so far as he becomes a subject that he discovers the ultimate subject within the historical, the subject that we call God. It is not in order to introduce any new techniques that we are taking on some of the challenges of this kind of theology, although the techniques and methods add in many ways to the theological universe as a whole. That man can only be social because he is cosmic and can only be historical because he is social is more basic than method.

Taking, therefore, this subject-object dialectic for mankind we can in fact discuss in the Irish situation how far we are historical objects and how far we are historical subjects; how far we are determined by historical, social and cosmic forces and how far we determine them, express ourselves through them, master them and so in and through them encounter the ultimate subject, God.

This raises of course the immediate problem that when we talk about history and then move on to talk about man as historical, we are usually thinking of the past. We are thinking of what has been done to us rather than what we have to do, and this is classical object thinking. If, in fact, we think of the historical condition of man as simply observing what has happened to him to date, we can only see ourselves as objects. The historical condition of man is much more directed towards the future than the past when we talk about man as subject. Even when we study past societies and past individuals we can think of them when they were making the future and not reflecting the past. This has particular relevance for

Ireland because there is a great deal of confusion about how far we are the objects or the subjects of our own history in Ireland : the value of tradition, rewriting our past history in order to eliminate any justification for the IRA or in order to forget or root out of our memory some of the ideas that might now prove troublesome or divisive. But this is not the way the subject deals with his past. There are 'subversive memories', to use a phrase of J.B. Metz, that keep coming back to impose on our peace. So we have to take our past seriously as the source of both creative and destructive forces in order to endorse the creative and somehow filter out the destructive.

## *Encountering God in History*

In dealing with this question of becoming the subject of our history and so finding God in faith we are not talking about an abstract process. We are talking all the time about people. History is not separable from people. It is not an idealised development process into which they are inserted. The forces of interrelationship that through the generations provide us with our present structures may make it seem like this. But it is in the interchange between people that this history exists. And it is in that interchange that we discern the Lord of history who is the meaning of history and the power of history and the liberating force in history : the Lord who was discerned in Israel and called by Jesus Christ, Father. We find him indirectly in our history because we are not capable of a face-to-face relationship. And we find him in the subjects of history, the subjects we call men and women. So that our awareness of and encounter with him, our faith, is in the movement with and towards the other humans in whose history we are involved, as they are involved in ours.

## *Universal Dimension*

It is not possible simply to confine ourselves to this island. We are engaged in a much broader enterprise, cosmic, social and historical. And the opportunities for becoming subject or the threats of remaining object do not originate simply in our own island but in fact are world-wide. So our recent awakening to the third world is more of an enrichment for us in the possibility of dis- covering God in those deprived people than it could ever be for them. And so of course on the reverse side the existence of the consumerist in us through a certain capi- talist structure, a certain materialist attitude to life threatens us, making us remain as objects. We share these wider opportunities, these wider limitations. And we have to struggle not simply alone but within the wider world to overcome these, to reduce the objectivisation of history. We can never become subjects on our own as individuals or even as a society. We are now in the 'global village' situation. Although this is only partially realised, the interaction is increasingly world-wide. We cannot therefore, even as Irish theologians reflecting on the condition of the Irish people in search of a fuller faith as subjects of their history, confine ourselves simply to distinctive Irish problems, and yet we have to look on the Irish problems. For the remainder of this paper I will look again at some of the Irish problems and then at one or two examples of more universal problems as they occur in the Irish context.

*Irish History*

There are two basic versions of Irish history: one written by the nationalist tradition and one by the unionist. There is a considerable convergence of these traditions among the scholars but there is considerable divergence in the mythical understanding at the popular level. Within the nationalist version the movement of liberation has two strands or perspectives: the constitutional perspective and the violent revolutionary one. I want to take a couple of instances from that past to show how the movement of history shows the change from object to subject thinking and achievement.

That happened, for example, under O'Connell—not for nothing was he called the Liberator. He was a pioneer in Europe, of such interest to Europeans that Montalembert came to visit him as a man who had found the key to combining Christian faith and the new democratic insight that people should be architects of their own destiny. O'Connell's movement had some remarkable sub-themes: his opposition to the proposed introduction by the British Government of the Veto on episcopal appointments and to the government endowment of the Irish Catholic clergy. This generated a lay movement that got the Irish bishops to change their minds so convincingly that they actually refused Roman directives on the matter and held out for emancipation without these ties. Here was a man organising an illiterate, still poverty-stricken mass of people in a powerful movement, carving out a destiny of its own. The people became the subjects of their own history.

Parnell and the Land League had similar influence. The revolutionary movements had also some of that kind of significance. There's no doubt that in the aftermath of 1916 the people's sense of identity has been strongly reinforced, people accepting their destiny to be self-governing people—the communal sense of being a subject of history.

### Subjectivisation, Ambiguity and Subsequent Objectivisation

This was done within the ambiguity that affects all historical achievements : it did not bring all the Irish people with it and still has not. There was a whole section of Irish people who could not see this as their destiny, who could not see this as making them the subjects rather than the objects of history and that difficulty still remains with us. And that is why you have two versions of history and two states in this island. This subjectivising was aided by the involvement of the Church and seen by people like Pearse as having a deeper Christian significance. However, not only is this subjectivisation of history riddled with ambiguity but when it reaches a certain stage of achievement it objectifies, stagnates and subsequently enslaves. In the Republic, we have to a large extent become objects again of that history. I may anticipate by pointing out that in so far as this applies to Northern Ireland, the real problem is that the two basic communities are objects of history. In their different and often violent ways they resent and react against each other because they are unable to find a way of being subjects together. And they can only be subjects together as architects of the history of the island.

*Northern Ireland*

For anybody in Ireland the most obvious and critical problem remains Northern Ireland. It is a problem of life and death, a problem for politicians, for all Christians. In approaching it the kind of critical faith analysis we should be doing must go far beyond either the simple moralising that condemns violence and endorses the very admirable peace movement, or the simple call on politicians to solve the problem. A good deal of theological reflection should be devoted to this problem, reflection not simply concerned with Church activity but primarily with the people involved in this situation.

I wish first to discuss the paramilitaries, because they are the people who highlight the problem. They are the most obvious people involved. And I wish to discuss them in so far as I believe that they come out of historical traditions that were designed to serve subjects, to make people subjects, traditions which because of their stagnation have rendered these people objects, objects in their political goals, in their attitudes to other people, and of course in their political methods. They are stuck with this stagnant tradition. It does not seem to me to be a question that can be answered at the moral level— whether what the IRA are doing today is justified in terms of what the people of 1916 did, any more than what the UDA are doing is justified in terms of what the people of 1912 did. One can see in 1916 and 1912 an element of the subjectivisation of their history which seems lacking today. The paramilitary movement is not leading anywhere in the sense of engaging the divided peoples in achieving a history for themselves. The goals or objects they are talking about—getting the British out or keeping the British in—are objects that belong to fifty or seventy years ago, but not today. Becoming the architects of their own history today is quite a different task from what it was then. And in the meantime new techniques and methods have been developed which could in the Irish situation promote this common achievement of their destiny in a human, subjective way and one not open to violence. It is not, again, necessary to enter into how far violence is justified in Latin America or Northern Ireland. A different analysis of each situation is called for and violence is not the way for the people of Northern Ireland to find their historic subjectivity in the short or long term.

There is reason to hope. Many of the politicians have made very brave efforts to escape the historic objectivisation. O'Neill, Faulkner, Craig are people who emerged from the objectivisation of their history and assumed some fresh subjective stance by meeting and understanding the people from whom they were alienated. From Nationalist to SDLP (Social Democratic and Labour Party) illustrates the same process. Limited in numbers and limited in quality these may be, but they and others—in the Alliance Party for example—do exist. At the popular level the latest manifestation has been the Peace People. At the Church level you can see the regular—some might say routine—statements on violence, calls for peace, and the various ecumenical moves that led to the Ballymascanlon meetings. However, we are still far from the breakthrough that would enable us as Christians together to be the subjective creators of our future destiny. We have not reached the critical point or the threshold of that breakthrough. When that

happens it will be the Revolution—if you like, the Resurrection. It is at that breakthrough stage, that death and
resurrection stage, that Christians will be able to hold
up their heads again, because in the historical process
that is now Ireland's shame (objectivised) and could be
Ireland's glory (subjectivised) they will have encountered
the ultimate subject of this history, the God of Jesus
Christ.

It might be worth developing another time how far
the Churches are slaves of their 'Catholic' or 'Protestant'
ethos. In so far as they are, they have allowed themselves
to become the objects of their history and cut themselves
off from their primary subjective call to be sons of the
Father and brothers of one another. The denominational
allegiances in Ireland are not pure faith allegiances.
They never could be. But how far they are the product
of a stagnant religious and cultural tradition which now
enslaves, merits serious self-examination on all sides. An
Irish theology of liberation would have to deal seriously
with the liberation of the Churches within their own
traditions and the liberation of their theologies. A liberation of such Irish theology as exists may be the first task
of an Irish theology of liberation.

## Some Other Irish Challenges

There are many groups of people who are far more
the objects of their situation and their history than they
are the architects of their destiny. In this, account must
be taken of the different aspects of the cosmic and social
and historical process. At the cosmic level one needs food
and warmth and shelter. At the social level one needs a
function in society, acceptance through relationships,

and structures to protect and promote all responses to these needs. At the historical level one needs a share in decisions about one's own future. A great many people are comparatively deprived at many of these levels: unemployed / employed; employee / employer; aged / young; ill / healthy; illiterate / educated. Even geography from east to west and from north to south in Ireland and in the world at large can be a source of privation. And there are people who are not only deprived but who scarcely emerge at all. Some have begun to emerge more recently like the travelling people, the battered wives, the one-parent families; prior to that there was the emergence of the handicapped and the alcoholic. Prisoners and homosexuals are still very much submerged. These are people who have to find the God of Jesus Christ through their historical existence and therefore have to be enabled to be subjects of their own history, and how little our society is concerned with that. Where it is, much of the action is no longer in Church bodies or with churchmen in Ireland; it is usually with groups like AIM or Cherish or the various Liberation and Civil Liberties groups. These are people who are concerned with the subjectivisation of our people, that they may achieve some liberation. And in the long run this liberation is necessary so that they may have the opportunity to discover in their lives, relationships and history, the God of Jesus Christ, that they may enjoy his hope in the historical enterprise of their lives and that they may share his presence in the supportive love of the narrower communities to which they belong.

*The Sexual Subject*

In discussing more general issues I might start with the cosmic area of ourselves: sexuality. We have paid very little attention to the historical subjective aspect of sexuality as constitutive of its human and Christian meaning and so of our moral tradition. It is in so far as our sexuality enters into our subjective engagement in history with others that we are as Christians chaste, mature sexual beings. And in so far as our sexuality is not integrated, it is sub-human, sub-Christian and the basis of immorality. This we have not really faced in our discussion of sexuality. A great deal of moralising tends to encourage the objectivising of sexuality. The whole tape-measure, 'how far can you go?' approach to chastity, now happily in retreat, was both impractical and destructive. No such measurement was possible. And the attempt or project ignored the subjective and historical and turned the person and his sexual dimension into an object, the ultimate immorality. It is in the historic search for meaning as a sexual subject through encountering, in a genuinely personal and subjective way, other sexual subjects, that one identifies and integrates this self sexually and so can respond lovingly and appropriately. This is the road, despite occasional mishaps, to human and Christian chastity.

The objectivisation is not an individualist thing. It is part of society and its forces. This is seen in the continued discrimination against one sex, a very good paradigm for liberation or salvation. Men cannot be fully subjects of their history as males without women being fully subjects of their history as females. Man's liberation is essentially part of woman's liberation.

*Conflict, Reconciliation and Historical Subjects*

Uneasiness with conflict is a very widespread clerical if not Church phenomenon. We might reflect on the matter in gospel terms—there would not be any reason to love our enemies if we had no enemies. So we must take seriously the question of conflict in the Church, in the family, in the wider society. We must not in the face of that conflict look for easy reconciliation, because it could be at the cost of people ever becoming genuine subjects of their history. We must not look for cheap peace in that sense. (And this is quite a different point from that being made by the Peace People, in case there is any confusion.) There is always a temptation to seek or accept an easy reconciliation. Experience with marriage breakdown makes clear the danger of that. Sometimes the cause of permanent marriage breakdown is easy reconciliation in the beginning. (In Ireland where all the pressures have hitherto been towards keeping the couple together at any price, with easy talk of reconciliation, there could be a swing to the other extreme where reconciliation would be regarded as impossible from the beginning.) Easy reconciliation breathes an easy optimism about one's difficulties. Optimism is not to be confused with Christian hope, which is born near to despair, and yet triumphs over despair. Christian hope is a hope at risk, on trial, constantly threatened. There is a paradoxical illustration of this.

We have already discussed how distrust between people breeds distrust. We have grown up in the Christian wisdom that love leads to love. And yet there is an inescapable human fact that is not sufficiently faced up to by the Latin Americans or any other theologians: that love at a certain stage breeds rejection; it even provokes rejection. This gives some measure of the sinfulness of man, of the deep-down object he is in regard to his history, that he is provoked to hatred or rejection by love. The classical instance occurred with Jesus Christ. What he provoked ultimately in his own people was this rejection. This tragic element at the heart of human existence is something that is very difficult to cope with, impossible to understand, and yet undeniably real. It is for me the dissolution of all cosiness about final achievement of the kingdom within history. It emphasises the puzzle of what human achievement and subjectivity means and yet the belief that there is no other way to God except in and through them.

## Prayer and Providence in Irish Theology

This engagement in history is really a discovery of God, a growing awareness of God, even a prayer awareness of God. In the Irish context there are a few points we should remember, partly for our own comfort, and partly for our discomfort. We belong within the European tradition. The distinctive Irish element is perhaps the simple immediacy of Irish prayers. This is to some extent still with us and has surfaced afresh in the charismatic movement. Yet there exists a real danger that we will encourage a childish form of prayer. There must be an adult prayer, not necessarily complex but it has to be real for the grown-up Christian, and the only way to make it real is by becoming an historical subject engaged in the human enterprise personal, Irish and global. Otherwise prayer becomes evasive and cheap, as an opting out of that enterprise and that subjectivisation.

The same kind of danger occurs in the Irish attention to Providence which we accept or give thanks for—or concede in our apathy that 'it will be all the same in a hundred years'. In the new movement there is a simplicity about Providence that is again heartening and hopeful. Yet it is also threatening, because there is a frightening temptation to simplify, to the point of saying: 'I opened the book at this passage and therefore I must do this' and so on. In the kind of engagement humans are involved in we have only got the half-light. We move forward uneasily between the sand traps. There is no easy way of recognising and discerning the will of God. Above all Providence is not something unrolling before us but a call to create the right kind of human history.

*Conclusion*

As has been pointed out elsewhere in this book the Latin American theology of liberation presents an exciting challenge to theologians everywhere, including Ireland. Perhaps the only useful contribution of this essay has been to experiment with their categories of history in terms of subject and object in the laboratory of Irish life and Irish theological reflection. The success or failure of the experiment and the fidelity to these original categories are less important than the stimulus it may give to other theologians in Ireland or similar theologically 'dependent' countries to undertake the urgent task of thinking through their faith in their own living situations. For the basic stimulus and continuing insight we owe a great deal to the Latin Americans.

# Select Bibliography

Alves, R., *A Theology of Human Hope*, New York: Corpus, 1969.

Assmann, H., *A Practical Theology of Liberation*, London: Search Press, 1975; U.S. title: *Theology for a Nomad Church*, Maryknoll, New York: Orbis, 1975.

Camara, H., *The Church and Colonialism*, London: Sheed and Ward, 1969; Denville, N.J.: Dimension, 1969.

*Christians for Socialism*, Maryknoll, New York, Orbis, 1976.

Davies, J. G., *Christians, Politics and Violent Revolution*, London: SCM Press 1976; Maryknoll, New York: Orbis, 1976.

Dussel, E., *History and the Theology of Liberation*, Maryknoll, New York: Orbis, 1976.

Ellacuria, I., *Freedom Made Flesh*, Maryknoll, New York: Orbis, 1976.

Freire, P., *Pedagogy of the Oppressed*, London: Penguin Education, 1972; New York: Seabury, 1971.

Geffré, C. and Guttierez, G. (eds.), 'Liberation and Faith', *Concilium*, June 1974.

Gremillion, J., *The Gospel of Peace and Justice*, Maryknoll, New York : Orbis, 1975.

Gutierrez, G., *A Theology of Liberation*, London : SCM Press, 1975; Maryknoll, New York : Orbis, 1973.

Kee, A., *A Reader in Political Theology*, London : SCM Press, 1974; Philadelphia : Westminster, 1974.

Lehmann, P., *The Transfiguration of Politics*, London : SCM Press, 1975; New York : Harper and Row, 1975.

Metz, J. B., *Theology of the World*, London : Burns and Oates, 1969; New York : Seabury, 1969.

Míguez Bonino, J., *Revolutionary Theology Comes of Age*, London : SPCK, 1975.

Moltmann, J., *The Crucified God*, London : SCM Press, 1976; New York : Harper and Row, 1974.

Peruvian Bishops' Commission for Social Action, *Between Honesty and Hope* : Maryknoll, New York : Orbis, 1970.

Segundo, J. L., *A Theology for Artisans of a New Humanity*, 5 vols., Maryknoll, New York : Orbis, 1973-74.

Segundo, J. L., *The Liberation of Theology*, Dublin : Gill and Macmillan, 1977; Maryknoll, New York : Orbis 1976.

Wren, B., *Education for Justice*, London : SCM Press, 1977; Maryknoll, New York : Orbis 1977.